A Spiritual Journey With

ZEMKLA

Interplanetary Avatar

Hal Wilcox
Carlos Allende

SAUCERIAN PUBLISHER

ISBN: 9781-955087032

© 2022, Saucerian Publisher

Al rights reserved. No part of this publication maybe reproduced, translate, store in a retrieval system, or transmitted in any form or by any means, electronic, mechanical, photocopying, recording or otherwise, without prior written permision from the publisher.

Hal Wilcox

Introduction

California has been the melting pot and breeding ground, where the ingredients of what would come to be known as the New Age were melted and mixed. Here, the spirit mediums entered in contact with beings from space. One of these mediums was Hal Wilcox. Not too much is known about Wilcox's works and his whereabouts. He did not get too much publicity like George Adamski or George Van Tassel. He did not appear in flying many saucer congresses like Van Tassel's Giant Rock Interplanetary Space Convention, nor did he often appear on TV or radio programs.

Hal Wilcox was a contactee, channeler and a seer. As a child, he had several psychic experiences.. He was the founder of the Institute of Parapshychology, later named The Universe Society Church (UNISOC) in Los angeles, California. Wilcox was the first white man to entered the Oriental Temple of Tenrikyo in Japan following the instructions given to him by other wordly being. This being later identified himself as Zemkla. Zemkla, man who governs planet Selo, in the Bernard Star system. Zemkla met Wilcox in 1961 and gave him certain data that was recorded, typed out and became a "Log Book" for the events that will ocurr in the following years. According to the information received over the years by Wilcox, humanity's goal is governance, wherein all the people of this galaxy are to learn via reincarnation and karma to live according to God's spiritual laws. This is the story of those amazing days when all begun.

Saucerian Publisher was founded with the mission of promoting books in Science Fiction. Our vision is to preserve the legacy of literary history by reprint editions of books which have already been exhausted or are difficult to obtain. Our goal is to help readers, educators, and researchers by bringing back original publications that are difficult to find at a reasonable price while preserving the legacy of universal knowledge. This title is an authentic reproduction of the original articles printed text in shades of gray. **IMPORTANT**, although we have attempted to maintain the integrity of the articles accurately, the present reproduction has missing and blurred pages, poor pictures from the original scanned copy. Because this material is culturally important, we have made it available as part of our commitment to protect, preserve and promote knowledge in the world.

This title includes the following pieces;
1. **PROLOGUE**
2. *A Spiritual Journey With Zemkla. Space Avatar*
3. **Hal Wilcox Through Newspaper Articles (1951-1993)**

Great, but unpretentious, this edition is a rare symbol by itself of what was going in the dawn of the modern UFO phenomena.

Carlos Allende
Editor, 2022

TABLE OF CONTENTS

PROLOGUE   i

A Spiritual Journey With Qemkla, Space Avatar   1

Hal Wilcox Through Newspaper Articles
(1951-1993)   58

PROLOGUE

Hal Wilcox: Early Years

California has been the melting pot and breeding ground, where the ingredients of what would come to be known as the New Age were melted and mixed. Here, the spirit mediums entered in contact with beings from space. One of these mediums was Hal Wilcox.

Not too much is known about Wilcox's works and his whereabouts. He did not get too much publicity like George Adamski or George Van Tassel. He did not appear in flying saucer congress like Van Tassel's Giant Rock Interplanetary Space Convention, nor did he appear on TV or radio programs. However, based on his publications and newspaper articles about him, it is possible to have an almost complete biography.

According to the Ancestry.com site, maybe Hall Wilcox was born in Conesville, Ohio, around 1936 to 1937. In 1952, Wilcox attended the Conesville High School, Conesville, Ohio. It seems that by 1950, Wilcox was living with his family in Conesville, Ohio. He relocated to Southern California in the late '50s. However, it is essential to point out that people with a similar faces can have similar names.

Harold Wilcox
in the U.S., School Yearbooks, 1900-1999

	Detail	Source
Name:	Harold Wilcox	
Estimated Age:	Abt 16	
Birth Year:	abt 1936	
Yearbook Date:	1952	
School:	Conesville High School	
School Location:	Conesville, Ohio, USA	

- Add or update information
- Report a problem

Taken from the Conesville High School Yearbook 1952. Page 88. Wilcox is number 26 in the second row. Conesville, Ohio.

FOOTBALL TEAM

First Row (left to right): Freddie Frye, Jim Crouso, Robert Braswell, Earl Shurtz, Robert Hoobler, Francis Hinds, Eugene Blair. *Second Row*: Roy Self, Assistant Coach, Raymond Gardner, Manager, Jim Ronshausen, Harlan McCleary, William Powell, William Gladstone, Harold Wilcox, Bill Wiggins, Dale Baird, Ralph Hampton, Paul Hothem, Jim Davis, Coach. *Third Row*: Russell VanSickle, Harold Easter, Dean Rehard, Dale Gress, Jim Norman, Jerry Legge, Robert Treasure, James Rhodes, Hadley Burton, Floyd Gress, Earl Eckelberry, Manager.

Taken from the Conesville High School Yearbook 1952. Page 88. Wilcox is number 26 in the second row. Conesville, Ohio.

Hal Wilcox

U.S., School Yearbooks, 1900-1999

Detail   Related   Source

Name	**Hal Wilcox**
Estimated Age	Abt 20
Birth Year	1937
Yearbook Date	1957
School	Los Angeles State College
School Location	Los Angeles, California, USA
Yearbook Title	Pitchfork Yearbook

Hal Wilcox

Taken from the Los Angeles State College Yearbook 1957. Los Angeles, California

phi mu alpha

Phi Mu Alpha, a Sinfonia Fraternity of America, made important advances in the promotion of the cause of music during the year, and also succeeded in its other aim, the promotion of the brotherhood of students of music.

Originally organized at LASC as the Orpheus Club, Phi Mu Alpha held two concerts during 1956-57 — concerts open to all students — and also held a series of social functions.

Smiling still at "three o'clock in the morning." And "when the saints come marching in."

FALL	OFFICERS	SPRING
Chris Pontrelli	President	Chris Pontrelli
Jim Weiler	Vice President	Jim Weiler
Charles Williams	Rec. Secretary	Harold Hale
Charles Williams	Cor. Secretary	Charles Williams
Richard Froton	Treasurer	Richard Froton
Dale Ziegler	Historian	Dale Ziegler

Chris Pontre[lli]

Hal Wilcox

Through their leadership many musical events were accomplished at LASC.

Vito Susca

Henry Chal[...]

John McRae

Gordon Bensel

Frank Wamp[...]

Harold Hale

Jack Echols

Robert Pow[...]

Phi Mu Alpha Sinfonic Fraternity of America. Taken from the Los Angeles State College Yearbook

1957. Los Angeles, California

Taken from the Los Angeles State College Yearbook 1961. Los Angeles, California

Hal Wilcox in the News

This section mentioned the articles in which Wilcox has been appropriately identified. In 1961, Wilcox graduated from the Los Angeles State College with a Bachelor's Degree in Arts. Wilcox did not exist to the American public until 1964 when he attended a five-day convention of the Borderlands Science and Research Associates at Harmony Groves in Los Angeles. Wilcox talked about his three years of experience in a monastery in Japan.

The Amalgamated Flying Saucers Club of America held a three-day convention in Reno, Nevada, in July 9-11, 1966. Wilcox was one of the final speakers who opened and closed his presentation with a mystic chant (do not forget that he was a music teacher). During the event, he tried to sell his booklet: Gateway to Superconsciousness. The publication is based on his knowledge in an oriental monastery and his subsequent space trip to a planet called "Celo". According to Wilcox's, the hallucinogenic drugs were brought to earth by extraterrestrials 500 years ago and given to the native Americans. While visiting "Celo", the space being gave him a vegetable with the same effects as LSD, but without drawbacks. His booklet deals mainly with drugs such as mushrooms, peyote, mescaline, and "plants from other planets". Also, this publication covers the method and way of life that Wilcox teaches at his Institute of Parapsychology in Los Angeles.

During the mid-'60s, Wilcox lived in San Rafael, California.

Hal Wilcox
in the U.S., City Directories, 1822-1995

Detail	Source
Name:	Hal Wilcox
Residence Year:	1966
Street Address:	H Av Apt 3
Residence Place:	San Rafael, California, USA
Publication Title:	San Rafael, California, City Directory, 1966

Taken from Ancestry (2022)

During the '70s, Wilcox was around Southern California giving lectures on several topics. On July 30, 1972, he talked at the Brookside Country Club in Los Angeles on "mediums, clairvoyance, and telepathy." Also, on October 1, 1972, he lectured on "secrets of ESP and how to utilize your psychic energies" at the Oakwood Club House in Los Angeles.

In 1973, Wilcox addressed the Professional Writer's League meeting with a talk entitled: "Secrets of ESP and how to utilize your psychic energies" at the Holland House in Los Angeles.

The Times-Advocate (Escondido, California) on July 6, 1974, reported that Hal Wilcox, president of the Parapsychology Institute in Los Angeles, gave a lecture on "Healing technique" at the Inspiration Hall in Escondido, California. The news also mentioned that Wilcox graduated from Santa Monica City College and held an architectural engineering degree. This is a piece of contradictory information from our findings on Wilcox. The news pointed out that Wilcox claims that he was sent, in an expedition, to the Yucatan Jungles, where he found "emerald tables" under a Maya Temple at Chichen Itza.

Wilcox attended the 1977 Van Tassel's Giant Rock Space Convention in Landers, California. Reporter Jan Cleveland interviewed him from the Sun-Telegraph at the convention. Wilcox mentioned that he works for MGM Studios in special effects for the T.V. series Logan's Run. However, there is no Hal Wilcox in the IMDB database, in the web under special effect, for the Logan's Run Tv Series for 1977. Wilcox claims that he was first contacted psychically by an individual called Fehsz in 1952. The method used by Fehs was entered Wilcox's body while he was in a trance and spoke through him. During trance or channeling (as known in UFO circles), Wilcox was told to go outside where he saw a bell-shaped craft hovering over East L.A. In the next meeting with this space being, he was told to find others like him who had also been contacted. His efforts led him to Japan, where he found a group of people who followed an ancient religion based on an early space contact. Later, He relocated to Hollywood. Here in Hollywood, a man like Burt Reynolds knocked at his door, and he was Zemkla. Zemkla gave him information on a blood platelete called "an indle" that can be used to developed psychic abilities. The next step in his endeavour was to establish a laboratory to develop super vitamins called "plobiums". After this, Wilcox was send to Yucatan, Hawaii, Zurich, and Japan. Finally, he said that he had traveled to Zemka's planet, Sello, and that the space being accompanied him to UFO conventions. Finally, he was interviewed in the now defunct Joe Pine TV Show. Several newspapers mentioned Hal Wilcox attending the 1977 Van Tassel's Giant Rock Space Convention.

In 1982, Hal Wilcox attended the Flying Saucer Convention sponsored by Daniel Fry's Undestanding Inc. Among the many speakers was "Hal Wilcox. A former school music teacher now in the motion picture business doing special effects". Wilcox told a reporter that he was trying to set up a combination of radio equipment and home computers to allow Earth residents to tune the Interplanetary Cultural Exchange that will link about 50 planets. He claimed that in October 1961 he contacted a space being called Fahsz outside his home in L.A. Fahsz used Wilcox's body to "trans channel" messages to earthlings. In 1964, Wilcox was physically taken from the Southern California Campus to Fahsz's home planet Selo.

In 1983, Wilcox gave a talk at the Church of The Inner Light in West Los Angeles entitled: "My physical UFO experince."

Reporter Alan Miranda interviewed Hall Wilcox at the UFO and Et conference held at Sedona, Arizona, in 1992.

Reporter Alan Miranda interviewed Hall Wilcox at the UFO and Et conference held at Sedona, Arizona, in 1992. Here is the transcript of the conversation:

Miranda:

Enrolling. Okay. Hi, this is Miranda Zannon. We're on location in Sedona at the UFO and Et conference, and I'm standing here with Hal Wilcox for 14 years, was an educator and school teacher, left that industry, went into the motion pixture business, doing special effects and experienced his first contact, the experience in 1961 and was followed up in 1963 by an actual physical contact. Now, what was the essence of the message that they gave you at that time? Why did they contact you? And how did that experience evolve?

Wilcox:

I was contacted because I was constantly asking questions from 1952 as to what's really going on on this planet. I was in a foxhole in Korea when I started asking questions and I didn't realize I was being guided or observed while I kept on asking questions. So as I asked questions, I got answers. It simply follows that way.

Miranda:

Now, do these answers come telepathically in the physical realm or what?

Wilcox:

Well, it started when I approached authorities and found out they really didn't know what they're talking about. I then started doing hypnotic regressions for two years. Then I learned how to go into a trans contact myself and contact the extended teachers. And for two years they came through me, my physical body, and then I channeled for six years. And at the end of the six years, we were told that this had been rebroadcasted through a physical device over the building, and we should go outside and physically see the device hovering over the building, which was a UFO.

Miranda:

And what did it look like?

Wilcox:

It looked like a flying saucer, a building type craft that's 33ft some across. And what Georgia Danskey successfully photographed for many years. This government says it's a swamp gas, of course.

Miranda:

Right. Well, what was the essence of the message that they gave you?

Wilcox:

My assignment was governance to see to America completing her third test of destiny, as started in 1774 in the home of Benjamin Franklin. Our first test was religious freedom. Our second was equal opportunity or rights. And our third test has to do with American heritage. Use it or lose it. So I've had to advance to seven projects in the last 40 years to come to this point.

Miranda:

Could you synopsize those projects?

Wilcox:

Yes. Project One was to find the others who had been contacted and see what the result was. In every case, they formed another religion, a world religion. Project Two was to explain to the scientific community what would happen if we allowed our indolent immune system to continue collapsing or if we enhanced it. The result is that we continue to let it collapse and we have AIDS, AIDS today instead of enhancing it and be stronger as rates. Project Three was to set up an all world radio network shortwave so we would have honest, good communication around the world of people speaking the truth.

Wilcox:

Project Four had to do with learning how to generate life force storage and use it something like you would understand electricity to power up and give what happened in Project Five artificial intelligence in a computer, which I then did project Five. Project Six, which caused me to leave the educational community and go into the motion picture industry, was to learn to put stories in pictorial form. So I put this entire story together and was shown on television coast to coast in the country of Japan because it was not receptive at all in the country of America.

Miranda:

And the name of that production was.

Wilcox:

Well, it was MTV Productions, and they have now shown the Truthful UFO story for the last 1015 years in the country of Japan. It's just now, as you're doing now, beginning to leak out to America.

Miranda:

People have the right to know.

Wilcox:

Yeah, but we have not received information. Various media have been clamped down on and not allowed to put out certain stories.

Miranda:

Why do you think that is control doesn't control by.

Wilcox:

Control, by misinformation or lack of information. And what's happening is as you are doing this, you are informing people now.

Miranda:

What about Project Seven?

Wilcox:

Project Seven has to do with American heritage in America's third test of destiny, which in both cases has to do with causing people to find out who they are, where they came from and what they came here to do and then wake up to that reality and then advance and be part of the already graduated 59 other graduate colony planets in this Galaxy. We all came here together and this is the last planet to graduate and we have not graduated now.

Miranda:

Is that akin to balancing inner and outer reality, so to speak, what goes on inside of us internally, our thoughts, our experience and the exterior?

Wilcox:

Well, it had to do with social more than anything else, to evolve a system of government whereby we would abide by spiritual law. And yet this government would be by and for the people is exactly what the United States started out to be. But unfortunately, today we're polluting it, selling it, burning and spitting on it, flushing it down the toilet.

Miranda:

And we only have a 38% voter turnout for the last presidential site. What does that tell you?

Wilcox:

Yeah, well, that's the whole point. If we were to take advantage of being an American in America, go to our public libraries while some of them still are open and use these things to learn, such as what you're doing. You're helping educate people in your own way. People would act differently. But unfortunately, the various medias are trying to keep information from the people and the people themselves. Now, who are pretty much brainwashed don't want to hear anything new because it would turn their religious thing upside. Red rock that's it.

Wilcox:

Rock the boat. And that's one thing we don't want to do is rock the boat with perfect or correct information.

Miranda:

And whether it be governmental culture, organizational, any corporate culture, any subject.

Wilcox:

So I'm one of these rare birds that was contacted physically, even as I lay my hand on your shoulder, physically contacted and given various assignments, which has caused me to travel around the world to various countries, to bring about conditions that have changed, not to be an evangelist or start another religion. That was my first project to make sure I did not start any more religions, but to try to share the truth and also to get certain things accomplished as which I've already enumerated to you. So right now, it's mainly to help people realize that once before we got so involved with high tech entertainment that we forgot who we were and what we came here to do.

Miranda:

Maybe we need to form edutainment rather than entertainment.

Wilcox:

Well, that sounds cute, but I think that's what the problem is that people are more involved with sitting in front of the boom tube and movies and things like that, et cetera, because I work with emotional industry. So I'm not going to slap or bite the hand that feeds me. But I think these tools can be used in a more effective manner as you are doing right this moment.

Miranda:

How bottom line, what's going to happen if we pay attention?

Wilcox:

Two things, we're going to come out of this thing the way it was intended by God and man on planet Earth, a successful nation, United States of America, and the other thing, we're going to destroy ourselves. We are going to self destruct. No one's going to do it to us. Your friends and my neighbors are going to help us self destruct.

Miranda:

Let's hope that doesn't happen.

Wilcox:

The other choice is that we postponed another year, perhaps.

Miranda:

Any personal advice you can give to our viewers that may be having some experiences that you've described.

Wilcox:

Yeah. I would suggest that people kind of wake up, not in a religious sense, but just pay attention to what's really going on. Bill Cooper came forward and tried to scare tactics, and I thought it would get everybody woke up, but it would scare the heck out of everybody.

Miranda:

And it didn't really do the job drove them further in the sand.

Wilcox:

Correct? Yes, sir. So I think that the word hope is awfully weak. So that's what I was saying inside here. I think that people have to realize there is a plan. It was laid out 3992 years ago, and it's very much enforced now and on course. But we have to continue with that plan until it's completed. And you're doing your bit in helping.

Miranda:

Thanks, Hal. How are you?

Wilcox:

I'm thanks for your nice talking to you.

Miranda:

And thank you.

The last-mentioned of Hal Wilcox in the news was in 1993. He was given talks at a local Dennys Restaurant in Los Angeles. At this time, he was living on Lexington Ave in Los Angeles.

Hal Wilcox
in the U.S., Phone and Address Directories, 1993-2002

Detail	Source
Name:	Hal Wilcox
Residence Years:	1994-1998
Address:	6153 Lexington Ave
Residence Place:	Los Angeles, California, USA
Zip Code:	90038-1761
Phone Number:	213-466-0519
View Neighbors:	View Neighbors

Taken from Ancestry (2022)

Wilcox's method & philosophy

Hal Wilcox, who had had several psychic experiences as a child, founded The Institute of Parapsychology, later named The Universe Society Church (UNISOC), in 1951. He was later ordained as a Spiritualist minister. In the early 1950s, along with several other individuals with mediumistic abilities, Wilcox learned of Master Fahsz and other ascended teachers of the Great White Brotherhood (termed TABOF or The Ancient Brotherhood of Fahsz). Wilcox and the other oracles began to channel messages from these teachers/masters who taught the group about the nature of the universe and humanity's role in it.

According to TABOF, the universe was created by God, described as "The Father, The Ultimate One, The Force behind All Force, The Ultimate Cause behind All Cause." God permeates the universe, which is divided into seven sectors. Our sector, under Master Brsgv, contains seven galaxies. Our galaxy is in seven groups of seven planets each, making a total of 50 principal colonies, including Fahsz's home planet of Narvon in the Altair system. UFOs are simply spacecraft used to colonize our galaxy and stay in touch with the inhabited planets or galactic colonies in the Milky Way. Shel services maintained contacts from 1951 to 1961, a method taught the group to facilitate regular communications. It consists of a brief ceremony where a mantra, "Ino Pazis Gnurum," is chanted, followed by a 30-minute message channeled by one of UNISOC's 12 oracles for directions. The short service, it is believed, activates the pineal gland, and connects it with either the INO, a galactic computer bank, of one of the space brothers within Fahsz's command.

In 1963 physical contacts started with Zemkla, a man who presides planet Selo, in the Bernard Star system. According to the information received over the years, humanity's goal is to govern all the people of this galaxy to learn via reincarnation and karma to live according to God's spiritual laws.

The Universe Society Church worked on seven Project Tests in the 50's. In completing the test projects, Wilcox discovered the results of past covenants, the first of which was a new Japanese religion, Tenrikyo. Since then, Wilcox has found many other teachings from the same source but presented according to humanity's changing cultural understanding. After the Church Project-1 in 1963, Wilcox was ordained as a Tenrikyo priest before moving to Project-2. While completing six projects, he wrote approximately 60 titles to expound the emerging truth.

Wilcox final days

We were unable to find any information about his death.

Interplanetary Avatar

Table of Contents

Introduction by the Author	1
UFO's over AMERICA	**3**
Ditman - Blanchard, First sighting	5
Report of sighting in Pasadena	8
A knock on the door	9
Report of the USC contact	10
USSR's CAPTURED DISK	**12**
The captive crew	13
The two-man device	16
Rockets, Russians & Spacecraft	19
Russian Flap '65	20
Alzura, Satan's Domain	21
REIGN of FAHSZ	**25**
Creation - Planetary Avatars	26
The Father's Commandments	27
Universal Law	28
Fahsz	29
Charts of Fahsz	30
Anahsz	31
MESSAGE from SPACE	**33**
Inside the Craft	34
Trip to planet Selo	36
VIMANAS from ATLANTIS	**43**
Atlantis at its height	44
Lemura - Nui	45
THE COSMIC BEING	**47**
Soul-mates & Twin-rays	48
Trial by Polygragh	50
Creed of Fahsz	52
PROJECT EARTH	**53**
The Institute of Parapsychology	55
Why Saucers in our Skies	56

Foreword

Spacecraft have visited this planet frequently during the last 6,250 years, awaiting the day when our planet could again be included into the "Council of Seven Planets". It is only since June 24, 1947 when Kenneth Arnold's sighting occurred that we as the New Agers have had interest in Flying Saucers and UFO reports. During our scientific growth men like Columbus struggle to bring new facts to the attention of the general populace and are considered "strange" or "mad" by the conformists. It may be too soon to speak of Interplanetary Cultural Exchange, as the main interest is WAR.

Just one year before Kenneth Arnold's historic sighting, this country was engaged in destructive atomic experimentation. Scientists were close to the inner secrets of the structure of matter. Delicately balanced instruments throughout this Sector of Space had been picking up atomic static due to our atomic detonation. It was not long before indications were pinpointed quickly to our Planet Earth as the group engaged in attempts to destroy matter. To our elder space brothers our scientific effort is only a minor static shown on their instument panels. The greatest concern of the "Council of Seven" is for the millions of human beings on this earth that could be killed because of a few unstable persons.

Writers and lecturers in the New Age field speak of a periodic polar flip. Such an event is not in the future; however, the basic concept is true. The big concern of this planet is to straighten up our differences here and now on this planet before we get off our island in space and carry death and bad manners out into space. Shooting first anything and everything that is not understood may not be the best approach to understanding.

Certain individuals on this planet have been selected as "possible contactees"; however, of these very few will do the "Father's work:. They are willing to look into the air and see the beautiful bell-type flying saucer, but no more. A great deal has to take place before we can expect reasonably spacecraft to come close enough and have social contact. As was my case, months passed before the small group and I met for the contact by way of "channeling" through my body while in trance. During these conversations many tapes of interesting information were recorded of our new space firends. As data increased, so did the number of persons that came to listen to the communications. From 1951 many pages of channeled communications from Spiritual Teachers and noteworthy individuals "on the other side" were recorded by the group. Since our only concern in this book is the physical ground to spacecraft contact, other topics will not be discussed. The Institute of Parapsychology is engaged actively in many other phases of investigation, "Project Earth" and class insturction.

The talks which were given were aimed at our spiritual growth and development, but underneath was an affair of greater importance. This unknown authority was identified later as ZEMKLA, Who knocked on my door in 1964. The data that neatly was recorded and then typed out became a "Log Book" of the events that led up to the major breakthrough which occurred in the following years.

As far back as 1957, I was told that there would be a specific man from another planet, Who would come here, land and physically make Himself known to me. When the trip to the Kanro-Dai device in Japan was over, I was contacted and according to Cosmic Plan a series of spacecraft contacts began. Although prior to the meeting I thought all information should be given to the people, it was withheld because the public would not have given it serious attention for two reasons: First, the Air Force was debunking all UFO sightings and, secondly, the information was for my personal spiritual development. For this reason, I was told to enter a monasterey, a place of quiet. I was the first white man to enter the Oriental Temple of Tenrikyo, where I lived and received the advanced teachings from members of TABOF after I was given all of the teachings of the piresthood.

Now, I have come out of the monastery and am at liberty to tell my story. I was instructed to guide as many as are serious along the pathway of the ancient truths that are still maintained by the "Church of the Universe" here on this earth. The stories that follow are completely true, and reports of the various flying saucer sightings are documented. Experiences seen by less than three adults will not be mentioned in this book.

UFOs over AMERICA

While we probe space and attempt to control the air traffic over America, we extend our view and discover that we, too, are being watched from outer space. The Air Force may not feel that it has our nation under military control unless every inch of "air space" is accounted for and protected. Top intelligence has to know exactly what is up there and who is behind it when they detect these solid machines. The Air Force, in its study of observations, has not found yet one act of a UFO attacking anything or anyone. The concept that this earth is just one of many small inhabited planets may cause some to feel as small fish in a very large pond.

With all the recent sightings of saucers by citizens of the United States, the fact that there are interplanetary space vehicles over America is an established fact. There is no need to push any panic botton - this is only an alarm clock set to wake up the people of the Planet Earth.

This group known as "Project Bluebook" has Major Hector Quintanilla, Jr. as the top director, and under him, Lieutenant William Marley. These men and others are in what could be called the G-2 Section of the Military Group. The original function was to combat through intelligence and force any group that infringed upon the security of the United States of America. The chain of command has covered many radar stations and interceptor commands all over the world. The objective in this country is to withhold facts which may endanger the common good of our United States. The control of the California Aeronautics Association and indirectly of the Associated Press and United Press as well as broadcast networks is allowing gradually the American public to learn of UFOs. In the face of the events of August 3rd, 1965, when MASS SIGHTINGS occurred on the "pathway" between the Los Angeles, California and Stonehenge, England, planetary vortices across the United States, it seems hard to believe that the Air Force could still withhold the obvious truth from the average thinking adult. Many persons swallow the stories of "runaway balloons", lightning bugs" for solid spacecraft even though their cameras produce clear photographs that do not resemble the "lamp post". Recently, when the major portion of the East Coast was in darkness, the people accepted the shallow answer which explained nothing - it appears that sleeping people do not demand explanations; only a pacifier and a story to lull the mind to sleep.

The policy in England and many other countries at the present, on handling the UFO information is one of general co-operation. The Director of Intelligence for Canada, W. B. Mith, saw fit to release a percentage of the UFO data to the press to "keep the public aware of the situation". With the unrest of America's youth, it is clear that truth, facts of life and reality, with a bit of discipline should at least be introduced to them.

There are two schools of thought within the officers of the Military Groups. They are: (1) Some believe our government is taking the wrong stand in withholding such vital information. (2) The other side demands all data be withheld from the public. At present there is practically no collaboration between civilian and military personnel nor between world governments. Surely somewhere between their extremes lies the correct action. The military, geared for war, is not able to cope (it seems) with the policy as it attempts to pass the buck onto some civilian agency. Exchange of UFO data is strictly on a non-military level and thus without a central control is very much like a chicken without a head. The hope is that common sense and basic facts that should be released by the Air Command will allow people to make a slow but rational adjustment. American citizens are learning the truth by seeing a UFO, which they are not prepared for, or through Flying Saucer Conventions are hearing of a larger and stronger voice saying, "Yes, UFOs are in our skies". This brings me to wonder what the Indians did when they saw the ships of the white men landing on the Eastern Shores.

Because of the reactions after the H. G. Wells radio production, "War of the Worlds", our government has just cause for concern for the welfare of the American public. Just to sit and be concerned since 1938 does not solve any problem. It is wise to consider the complete situation before leaping into action, yet acknowledgment of UFOs as a fact has not been made. These long years have brought the UFO situation to a head for the Air Force, as millions of our citizens are seeing the craft. The Air Force sits on a volcano of repressed "public information", and is trying now to pass the buck.

It may seem that the entire subject and issue is "seeing a flying saucer"; this is not true. Adjustments will have to be made in every aspect of our lives when social and economic exchange with another world starts. There are still some tribes or pockets of people on our earth that have not as yet had a chance to adjust to airplanes, cars and the modern world. These people (and others I would guess) would be very "upset" to learn of the advances on this planet, not to mention spacecraft from other worlds. Missionaries to remote tribes probably are regarded in the same way as the men and women from space would be regarded by Americans.

The important point, and main issue comes under the heading of "CULTURAL ADJUSTMENT". Imagine for a moment what you would encounter if you could visit our world just 100 years ago. Suppose you took with you several portable electrical devices from our society. As you tried to present the concept of aircraft, cars and the commonest of household appliances, you would risk the "ducking stool", being "burned alive at the stake", or a prison cell. All you could do is disturb a few of the people who dared to listen to what you said.

During the ever increasing UFO sightings the single point of importance is not the machine, but man himself. Fright and flight are the primitive drives of fear and today, often it is possible to release this by killing or destroying the object of the fear. Science has not as yet gained control of the various illnesses, so as a group we plod alone with primitive sanitation and health rules.

These same people give no thought as to whether their bodies could endure the flight. One of the first things that missionaries have to do is to start primitives on a program of health and sanitation and not frighten them. The basic concern is the human being and his ability to stay alive. The human being is the common denominator of the entire universe for cultural and scientific advance. If, we on this earth would dare to start health and sanitation practices NOW, it would be several generations before that first healthy child could be born into a healthy civilization. Even so, this should be started as soon as possible, as many of us are still alive and just might be able to adjust to healthy living. Our young people, through "Science Fiction", have adjusted their thinking so they can accept new and better ways of living. Others insist on no change, and the "good old way", although stagnation is certain death.

DITMAN - BLANCHARD, FIRST SIGHTING

This story begins on April 25th, 1961 in the city of Los Angeles, California, at 2:00 p.m. in my home. During the communication with Master Fahsz, contacted by "channeled control" through me and one of the students present, the subject of flying saucers was introduced. The request for a sighting was made directly to Master Fahsz to occur as soon as possible. This request, we learned, had to be relayed through a Sector Operations Officer before the request could be considered seriously. The next voice that was heard was that of the Sector Operations Officer. He started telling us of the air control problems and the general unwillingness of the UFO Captains to materialize over a populated area. Our hearts sank as he attempted to explain the situation.

We were told that they did not want to enter our "Time-Space Field", because of the recent trouble with both the American and Russian Governments, who were both very eager to capture a flying saucer. Policies had just been changed on the UFO subject, which resulted in orders for many craft to be returned to their bases and the craft in the range of radar and anti-aircraft guns to remain "out of range"

Asking the Captain of such a craft to place his craft over my house in full view to be seen by our group was not so exciting for those aboard. We were told that should any military aircraft appear on the scene, they would have to move instantly a different "Time-Space Quadrant" and this would slow down our meetings, as their craft had remained aloft to relay communications. In later years these interceptions resulted in being landed many miles from where I had parked my car.

Upon further questioning the Sector Commander told us why they were unwilling to be <u>seen</u>. We were told that for our present understanding "Fuel-frequency" is the propelling force needed in the driving control. This fuel, although not tangible, force their craft, a tangible object, through space. When they don't wish anyone in one "Time-Space Quadrant" to see their craft, they move into another. The reverse of this is also true. By lowering their "Fuel-frequency" they can be seen and boarded. We also were told that once seen by radar scopes, this would act as a trigger reaction, activating our government's sternest and strictest orders about UFOs in 1961.

He went on to say that if our meeting was brought to an end at 2:00p.m. and we went out to the front of the house, within five minutes from that time a sighting of a flying saucer would occur. We were told that if we looked in the correct direction all would see it with our own physical eyes. At the time there were four spacecraft stationed in this area; this was one of that group. One of the students asked "Are any of these four aware of our effort right now?" The answer was, "Yes". This stunned those in the room, as we thought the entire proceedings were behind locked doors and secret.

Fact of the matter, the entire effort had been watched for the past few years, as the members of TABOF are trying to find people who are willing to work for the good of all God-loving men. Our group had followed the instructions and developed as it had been hoped, not realizing the importance of it all. The spiritual teachings that came through were such that all of the individuals in our group developed their own awareness. The purpose was that it was hoped that each would start his own group and continue the contacts in an ever enlarging circle.

Many attended these early contacts but only a few saw it through to the end and shared in the sighting, which ended the channeled contact and started the new physical contacts. It was very fitting that these should finally see the very craft that had done the transmitting all of these years.

The Sector Commander spent a great length of time explaining the situation to us in the attempt to make us understand that such a sighting was not important. At the end He told us, "Look Eastward, probably quite a distance, over a non-inhabited area at an elevation of 15 degrees above the horizon. Your group will be able to watch a scout craft move into clear view". He went on to tell us that this was one of the "two" that were having to wait! These it was learned later in 1964 was ZEMKLA, an Avatar from another planet in our group of seven planets. These men are the representatives of two other planets in the same group as Planet Earth, but not of the same solar system. The entire "Group Vll" includes three women and four men, who carry out the Will of the One Father, as related by the Sector Commander Fahsz. In all there are 49 Avatars in this sector, Who bring developmental data from the larger body, the "Sector of Fahsz" and introduce this to their own home planets as the "Interplanetary Cultural Exchange". They have a great deal of concern for every one of the forty-nine and therefore, have assigned seventeen people, 7 women, 10 men, each to help our Planet Earth. This minimum number of selected workers on the earth at present should be: 17 x 49 = 833, or 882 men and women, including all of the Planetary Avatars in the "Sector of Fahsz".

The scientific concepts, the indole discovery, personal development methods and general knowledge of the advanced way of life on Selo and other planets, is to be given to those people who will do work. It is not enough to just receive data, the material has to be put into condition so that it can be presented to our people, so they can understand the "method". These concepts were taught in the school of Metaphysical Arts and Sciences I founded in 1962 under the sign of the planetary conjunction.

The Institute of Parapsychology offered a 60-unit, two year course, both to teenagers and adults, as well as through a mail order course in monograph form. The purpose was to test the curriculum given by TABOF and develop teaching methods that will maintain stable and dependable results. The classroom situation allowed for a complete test, for it is impossible to predict success on the drafting board. The close observations of all students made it possible to adjust the teaching methods until we, as teachers, knew that ability which each student had, depending upon how many semester hours of work had been completed.

When the channeled contact ended, we went out in front of my home and tried to figure out which direction was East. We were told to look in the East for a scout-type craft, which is identified by the drawing on the cover of this book. The group was very excited as they, too, had never seen an honest-to-goodness flying saucer. I had seen them before, but they were so high that I could not be certain if it were an aircraft, comet or star, and at those times I did not have the ability to ask anyone to identify the unknown sighting. According to the communication, finally this sighting was to come about after so many hours of taped conversation, so we felt that it may be the turning point in our contacts. It was a wonderful thing to think at last we will see the very craft that has relayed communications all these years. Lastly, it would connect all of the data collected with physical reality.

After getting our bearings and searching the sky in the Eastern direction, we saw it! The flying saucer appeared in the distance as a point of light, looking very much like a tiny sun. As it approached not a word was uttered and the feeling was like "catching a fish". Eventually, it moved over our heads and we felt a little braver and began telling each other what we saw. The excitement was very much like children at Christmas. The happiness was great and we began to try out the various Air Force test, tongue in cheek. We compared the craft with a wild goose, a baseball and a pumkin and then rubbed our eyes, pinched each other's arms...the whole bit! Yet there it was! It was no street light. It was a beautiful bell-shaped saucer!

THE FACTS: Time/place of sighting: April 25, 1961, at approximately 2:00 p.m. local time/vicinity of East Los Angeles, California, above Ditman Avenue and Blanchard Street. Duration: 15 minutes. The number of observers: four adults. Type of observation: ground to air. Number of objects: one. Observer reliability: good. Shape: disk shape (Air Force classification). Dimensions: two car lengths across. Color: silvery bright. Sound: none. Altitude: Approximately 3,000 to 5,000 feet. Speed: first sighted at unknown speed; it stopped for 15 minutes and then darted upwards, speed unknown. Tactics: flight East to West, stopping overhead, then flying straight upwards. Comment: witnesses on the scene, UFO or flying saucer. The Air Force's general comment, without seeing the object, "swamp gas".

REPORT OF THE SIGHTING IN PASADENA

The second sighting occurred in the area of Pasadena, California, when a group met at the home of one of the author's study classes. The sighting of the previous day had just been described to the group, and because of the interest it produced, it was suggested that an attempt be made to contact the same spacecraft under further test conditions. The conditions set up by the group were: (1) WHEN the spacecraft should appear, (2) WHERE it should appear, and (3) exactly WHAT movements it would make after appearing.

The class went out in front of the house and Hal proceeded to make telepathic contact with the Captain of the spacecraft. When Hal was asked what he intended to do to cause the craft to come into view, he said, "I will try to hold in my own mind what it is that I want them to do, and after I have seen it in my mind, try to project it to them by the use of mental telepathy. However, remember this is a request, and I leave it entirely in the hands of the Operations Officer of this sector, whether the request will be carried out or not."

After a pause of some five minutes, a star was noticed in the area that had been selected to be shining brighter than any other around it. The location had been West and at a 30 degree elevation. This star or light was in that spot. No one spoke for a long period of time. Soon it grew brighter than any other around it. The location had been West and at a 30 degree elevation. This star or light was in that spot. No one spoke for a long period of time. Soon it grew brighter and brighter. It was acknowledged as not a star, but a spacecraft. It appeared just five minutes from the time selected and in the location previously agreed upon. The movements were from the original point to directly overhead, then a circle, and lastly, a triangle motion coming at a rest again directly overhead. Almost all were convinced that what we saw was a spacecraft under conscious control following our requests as closely as possible. There was one person, however, who still did not agree that there was any connection between our wishes and the movements it made in the night sky. So it was agreed that he decide what he wanted it to do and try to project that thought up to the craft. In a hasty minute he said, "Oh, I just wish it would go back to where it came from", and that is exactly what it did. It shot straight across the sky and disappeared in the general area where it had first appeared.

A KNOCK AT THE DOOR

Recently, I had returned from the Orient and my prime objective had been to develop the material that Zemkla and TABOF had given me over the years. I consolidated all of this material and "The Method" into a course of study. It was necessary for me to go to Tenri City, Japan, where I lived the life of a monk and receive these teachings without interruption. When I returned to Los Angeles, California, I then selected a location centrally located, using a two-story house as my office. The location was near Camerford Avenue and Vine Street in Hollywood, the heart of the motion picture business.

Actors pass by my office-house as a daily occurrence. It was not uncommon to see strangely attired persons pass by my office-home, especially dressed for Western scenes.

Looking out of my window one morning during a lull, I happened to glance up and saw a man dressed very much like a circus acrobat. I smiled to myself and wondered what set the fellow was working on. I didn't give it much thought and returned to my work only to hear a knock at my front door. It was the acrobat. I wondered what he could want and made a mental note of the locations of the different studios. I prepared to answer questions about directions to one of the various motion picture lots, which were within the immediate area of my home. I opened the door and said, "Yes?"

The reply to this query was startling. The acrobat opened the screen and stepped boldly into the room, turned and said, "I am Zemkla!" The man looked in every way my superior in strength. (At this I confirmed in my mind he was a circus athlete.) Before many more notions raced through my mind, I heard this man announce for a second time, "I am Zemkla!" This confirmed it. The fellow must be an Italian circus star and like so many others, has taken an unusual name. Again he said, "I am Zemkla!" He walked through the house to my office, as if he had been here before. Again he said, "I am Zemkla!" and extended his hand and said, "I'm glad to greet you". I felt that I had met him somewhere, but had forgotten his name. As I extended my hand he grasped it as well as my arm, much like a Roman soldier. He seemed to be doing something mentally while he held firmly to my arm. I felt as if my every thought was laid bare before him.

He told me that He is from Planet Selo, and has been sent to me under the direction of Master Fahsz. Probably He detected disbelief in my mind, because He asked me to step out in front on my home to prove His statement: 'That He had been sent from Planet Selo by Master Fahsz'. Zemkla made a few motions in the air with His arms, along with certain unusual vocal sounds. Above us a cloud parted and a beautiful bell craft such as on the book cover, shimmered in the light. As the spacecraft descended, He asked it it looked familiar. I said, "No". He told me later after we returned into the house that this so-called flying saucer was the same craft that my class had seen on April 25, 1961 at 2:05 p.m.

As He related the details of the Ditman-Blanchard sighting, I knew that He had to either be standing at my side, or in the craft that day. My doubts still showing, Zemkla raised His hands, chanted Ino-Pazis-Gnurum, and the smog cleared and the sun seemed to shine brighter. He told me that at a later time I would learn to do the same thing, as it is important the sun shine on the earth and does not become obstructed with the smog of Los Angeles. He told me that smog attacks human lung tissues and destroys the indoles, but it will be several years before our scientists recognize that "SMOG CAN KILL!" I felt a little relieved but shaken as we returned into the house. While I sat on the couch, He paced back and forth, talking about "PROJECT EARTH" and the assignments that have to be accomplished on this planet, intermingling His talk with interesting stories about His own planet.

Zemkla answered all of the questions that I asked and gave me an overview of the mission which He called "PROJECT EARTH". He outlined several of the classes that He wanted me to give to those persons who expressed sincere interest. I was told that it was very important that no one know where I got my information, for the data must stand on its own. After several of the most interesting hours Zemkla told me that He must go, so that I could put the course together. He said He would see me again soon.

It was in the last part of 1964 before I was contacted again. I was in the middle of some research work with LSD for the book "ESP FOODS"*, (which identifies which foods promote spiritual development, psychodelic experiences, and which so-called foods are indole poisons). Upon leaving the laboratory at the University of Southern California, I walked south to the parking lot on the west side of the Coliseum where I had parked my car. As I walked along the sidewalk, I noticed two men dressed in what appeared to me as motor cycle uniforms, walking in the same direction. I cut across the grass attempting to avoid them. In a short time they caught up with me and when they were close enough, I noticed that both wore the insignia of Fahsz on their sweaters. Around each neck was a medallion on a chain that was the "Seal of Fahsz" with several jewels in it. As we walked I tried to get some sort of a conversation going, but neither answered. Further along when I stopped and insisted on knowing who they were and where we were going, one of these men gave the same arm shake as Zemkla, and with it came a feeling of inner calm. He walked on across the lawn to the parking lot where to my complete surprise I saw a bell-shaped spacecraft right in the parking lot! When we approached the craft, I saw Zemkla and felt an inner joy and happiness, knowing I would again talk with my wonderful friend. Again we were aboard and the craft rose silently from the ground. Zemkla greeted me and I sensed that I was in for something very unusual.

After the initial greeting, the question I asked first was, "How was it possible for them to fly in and park in broad daylight and not be seen by the many people in that area?" I was then reminded by Zemkla that they did not pass through the air-space, but through inter-dimensional controls and overcame time-space. Our flight path was to the south, passing through the air just as an aircraft. The sensation was similar to the unexpected lifts felt when flying in an airplane; while the other method, overcoming time-space, caused the feeling of absolute rest. The results of our flight passing through the air-space, I learned once I was back on the ground, as mysterious unknown flock of ducks as the Air Force had so spotted.

*ESP FOODS - a textbook for a class by the same name, taught at the Institute of Parapsychology, in Los Angeles.

I told Zemkla of my surprise to have been greeted by other members of his crew while on the USC Campus. He told me that there were many other persons which have been stationed on this planet from Selo alone and that other planets of our "Planetary Seven" have also stationed a cultural exchange crew on our planet. Certain of these individuals have come here using the principle of reincarnation, others by spacecraft.

THE PYRAMID SANCTUARY

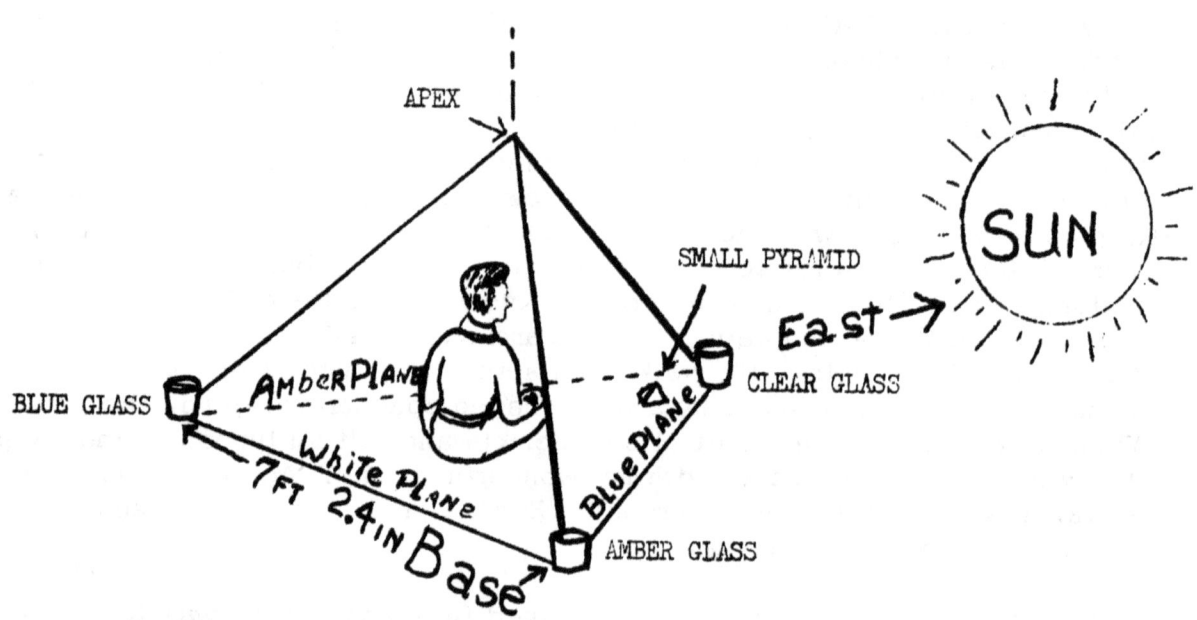

How to activate the Pyramid
1. Face east, sun, clearglass, envoke the God-force with prayer to manifest clear glass. (6 oz. water plus 1/32 teaspoon of Ginger)
2. Face to left, blue glass, extend force from clearglass to activate the blue glass. (6 oz. water plus pinch of Ginger).
3. Face to right, amber glass, extend force from clear glass to activate the amber glass. 6 oz. water plus pinch of Ginger).
4. Face west, bring amber and blue forces together, by prayer.
5. End activation ceremony by acknowledging East with a Thanksgiving for Life.
6. The meanings of glasses:
    Blue glass   Eiyadas force   Attraction - repulsion
    Amber glass   Eijira force   Atomic structure
    Clear glass   Hemlo force   God consciousness
7. Face Hemlo force when meditating; when working for another face west.

USSRs captured DISK

Union of Soviet Socialist Republics

In order to comprehend the flap of August 1965, it is important to go back into UFO history and bring to light perhaps the most significant event in UFO study to date. The event was first revealed to me in 1961 and at that time I was not allowed to reveal my communication with the spacecraft. There is still some question as to the reaction of presenting these facts both from those controlling the airspace over America and the general uninformed or more properly stated, "misinformed American public".

The following story is transmitted by way of tele-thought through myself, Hal Wilcox. It is the policy of the author to have everything tape recorded as it can later be studied.

Early in the 1960's there was a two-place spacecraft on a routine mission over the land area known as the United States of Soviet Russia. The crew had been assigned to keep tabs on the progress that had been made by the Russians as a result of taking over the many projects that Germany had developed during the Second World War in connection with rocketry. The ground contact men were ordered into the area at the close of World War II, and like so many others stationed on our planet live among the people for so many years that they had adapted the customs and language   These two men had surveyed the potential strength of the U S S R in controlling the placement of atomic devices delivered by long range rockets on a specific target. At the conclusion of their survey they were to report back to the mother craft, which during that time orbited the earth. The space-craft was of a special nature in that it was as small as possible and yet, large enough to hold two men. They hid their craft in the open area, or flatlands of Russia, where it remained buried for many years. When their project was finished they went to the hiding place and proceeded to leave the planet using their two-place device. As is the case with all physical creatures they must face the consiquences of physical entrapment. In this case the two men found that the craft was not in proper working condition that they had expected, and so although they could travel over the surface in the manner of a   "levi-pad-car"   (sometimes called a ground effects machine), they could not raise it high enough to re-enter the mother ship.

At this same time the counter-espionage people of the Soviet Government had themselves entered into a drama of their own. So, while these two gentlemen from another planet prepared to repair their device in what they thought was a completely unpopulated area the agents of Russia were keeping their activities under servailance. The two men went to a flat area out in the open so that they would be able to see if anyone attempted to approach them during the landing and repair operation.

as it happened, there was some minor damage so these repairs were started. Not only had they been discovered but followed every step of the way to their craft.

The policy within Russia today is such that unusual activities of people causes more than just interest, so when this repair started, due to the mechanical failure, the two male citizens form Selo were over powered and captured by the secret police of the Russian Government. The end result of this well-hidden drama was that they were taken prisoners, and their device was taken in a very secret manner back to the city of Vladivostok, and then on to Kiev, where they were given a very comfortable place to live with every convience, except one...freedom.

When the Sector Commander learned of their capture, he ordered them by tel-thought to comply with the wishes that the Russians imposed upon them. However, because the only interest the Russians had was in the direction of advanced rocketry, it would lead to nothing. The great data that they gave to the Russians was to them like revealing the secrets of playing "jacks", "marbles", or "hop-scotch". At the same time there was secret war going on between the Russian Government and TABOF, the combined efforts of all the people in our Sector of Space who observe the war-like tendencies of this planet. Although the results of the many space shots performed by the Russian Government ended with mysterious failure it could be traced to this single act of the capture of two men from planet Selo.

There were sudden changes of policies on the UFO's. Although only those who observed from above the planet realized the central cause. The Russians gained sudden data of a highly advanced nature about rocket propulsion. The members of TABOF made haste to remove all of the structures from the moon's surface and removed the mother craft from detectable range. The Allied Forces received a reversal in policy for UFO's from "observe them" to "shoot them down". Counter reactions begin to take place: The deployed spacecraft over atomic plants and other key positions were quickly ordered back to their home planets. The Russians started a frantic struggle to get on the moon by rocket power and the understanding of the two-place device they captured. The Allied Forces doubled and then tripled their efforts to "shoot something down"!

This game of wits was stalemated by removing all but four craft from this area of space. Earth men and women struggling to learn how to distroy matter, kill each other, enslave the God given freedom of man's soul, and his divine birthright.

THE CAPTIVE CREW

To be sure, the Selocians received the greatest consideration just short of their freedom. Each was assigned to a different scientist who have become their constant companion. For a period of time they were able to use their mental comunication in order to receive instructions from both their team captain as well as the Sector Commander. Soon however, due to eating the normal diet of uninformed persons living on this planet they lost their indoles and "seventh sense". Soon, with out the necessary supplementary "E S P Foods", they lost all of their abilities even mental telepathy. The instruction that they were given by the Sector Commander was to give the most primary answers to all questions asked. While these were aimed at rocket propulsion it was a recognized fact that rocketry is obsolete from a practical standpoint and thus no information at all. So, although the top Russian scientists gained a great quantity of information they gained nothing of vital nature.

During the early years of the confinement of these two space visitors, the Sector Commander directed others to contact the USSR Government and demand the release of these men. The only response that the Russian Government had was to describe the living conditions under which the two prisoners were living, pointing out that it was a life of pleasure. This provoked the Sector Commander who suggested that future moon-shots, which were the goals of the Russians at that time, would be caused to fail as soon as they attempted.

Two major changes took place due to this Russian attitude: (1) Bases then established on the moon were removed, as up to that time, according to accepted interplanetary practices, contact with the moon or conscious landing of persons on the moon would have led to face-to-face introductions to other members of our race,i.e., the human race from other planets. So the removal of these bases ment the removal of any oppertunity of being allowed into the Council of Seven Planets for any native of this planet.

(2) Non-violent orders were issued to the remaining members of the mission called "Project Earth". Removal of all but two craft were ordered from this planet. Although, as Americans we do not like the idea of being classified in the same grouping as the Russians, prior to this incident the American Government was contacted by planetary Avatars sent here specificly to invite our planet into Interplanetary citizenship. Repeatedly they made vain attempts to gain the co-operation of the American and Russian governments. However, no major world power would lower themselves to accept them as friends. The Russian Government captured their crew, and the American Government gave strict orders to "shoot them down".

Realizing that it was possible for a Interplanetary Karmic situation to start and become so entangled that there would be no hope for Earth. Earth Karma could drag down other "would be helping planets", so a higher level issued "hands off" orders so that those from Selo and Prismov would not become ensnarled in the Alzur forces of evil on Planet Earth. TABOF has always treated each and every governmental agency of this and every other planet with equal consideration, showing no favors and awaiting until all governments are of "one voice", TABOF must wait until the governments of Earth invite a deligation of officials from the Council of Seven Planets to come to this planet to discuss the admission of this planet into the Council of Planets.

The two Selocianprisoners have continued their lives within Kiev City under the "protection" of the Russian scientists. The exchange was a comfortable life for information of an advanced scientific nature. This continues to this day and accounts for many of the surprising advances the USSR has made these last few years. At the same time some thought should be given to the families of these unlucky men who are awaiting the eventual return of their husbands, sons, and brothers. Many a talk must have taken place around a fire-side as to the well-being of these two space travelers who are unfortunate enough to be living on planet Earth.

As the last planet in a series of seven groups of seven planets fourty-nine developed planets in all, our goal should be to overcome the alzur forces. Due to the constant struggle to learn new and better ways of killing people planet Earth has become the object of singular importance. Because we are the last of this sector to be admitted into TABOF we have drawn the attention of the citizens of the 48 planets under Fahsz's jurisdiction.

While the civic minded on these developed planets observe our actions still another organized group plan our downfall. There are others who work on the opposite side. The "Forces of Alzur", or the "Dark Ones". It is this group that shoot down our aircraft and sink ships to abduct humans for their own purposes. While complete ships at sea and now aircraft containing hundreds disappear practically no one realizes that the forces of Alzur need a quick and direct supply of human bodies on this last battle front of this sector of space.

Each planet of the Council of Seven Planets have had their due share of these Alzur forces and have overcome them, each in their turn. Now it is our turn. All eyes are on us to see what we will do. The forces of Alzur are among us, known as the "Dark Ones" (having no racial implications), because they serve the Black Angel who was banished from the Divine Kingdom, and who must try to confuse. Many helpers have come to our planet to assist us in our struggle with the forces of darkness, but they will only help, not do all of the work for planet Earth.

While they as planets have graduated into what we can only refer to as the ultimate civilization, and thus, caused the "great seperation". The great seperation starts with the removal of alzbrums from each of our bodies, and away from this planet. The struggle in Watts, California is just the begining of the battle of Revelation, which is a struggle to serve God or Mammon. Just as the control of the forces of Alzur is taught by the members of TABOF on a planetary scale they have released some of their teachings through which personal protection and control of the alzbrums is taught in the course, "Wisdom of The Masters", and the book,"Gateway". This seperation, or control of the Alzur forces, has caused the complete removal of all Alzur force from their planets where it has been released into space to drift into the next planetary system. We on earth are the last in this chain of 49 planets, and thus receive the Alzur force thrown off from Celo. So, as we move into our time of "seperation", souls who were not ready to rid their bodies of Alzbrums and remain in the "Golden Age" as it comes to their planet are being born on earth to take part in our "graduation". Some who incarnate here as students who have flunked out of every Planet school are being enrolled in the slowest of all planet schools...Earth. Along with them are many advanced teachers and helpers that have come to our Earth to help in this struggle. These souls now have their last chance to be marked as the chosen ones or will be sent on to the next school, outside the sector of Fahsz. It is for this reason that the Holy Men of the East cry out in anguish when a soul must be banished as this is the last planet school in this sector.

THE TWO-MAN DEVICE

The two-man device that was captured by the Russian scientists has now been successfully taken apart, piece by piece; the separate parts identified, drafted, and reproduced. Presently, and for several years now, the Russians have built more than one copy of the captured device. The USSR has manufactured these from their own plans; and have them ready for operation, as soon as they can understand the spiritual laws involved. All that holds them back, or has held them back, is knowledge connected with flight. This our government has known and because of this knowledge has left no stone unturned in the attempt to shoot down anything that resembles a UFO. Truly we cannot presume to know from whence the UFO came but it is generally accepted that they were from other planets, except for the Air Force, who still stick to the story of "super sonic flights of geese, street lamps, and swamp gas".

There is a space race on, but of a far more different nature than we citizens are told. Our governmental agencies had our best interests at heart throughout the UFO ordeal. But by having policies which keep us completely uninformed they have unwittingly paved the way for mass hysteria. Many people see and photograph those "super sonic geese". However, the photographs and drawings, are the same; not beach balls, super sonic pelicans, or swamp gas from Florida. Concern with command of the air-space over America has bacome so important and the swamp-gas investigators for the government are too busy to be concerned with anything of a planetary scale or scope.

Natural flights of devices that follow known patterns are of little interest or concern. However, craft traveling at 10,000 miles per hour, changing their direction at high speeds, and dematerializing in the middle of a flight path are of prime interest. If these are thought of as from another planet it will only be "more of the same", swamp gas. But if these are from Russian assembly lines--- a horse of a different color!

Every physical item on the persons that have been held behind the Iron Curtain has been throughly investigated for several years now. As much as could be learned has been instrumented into Russian scientific advancements. In a vain attempt to balance the scales many of the government scientists and military branches have been given advanced scientific knowledge. Information to test people to see how they would conduct themselves has been given to quite a few. These facts have been misused, misrepresented, and their respected contacts abused. It has been for this reason extremely important to find persons on this planet that can be honest and report what they have been given honestly. It was for this purpose that the author was contacted many years ago and given scientific truths, given tests, and told to with-hold this very exciting information for one reason, to test his truthfulness. For this reason he has been under for some nine years prior to this publication, secrecy concerning the continuous visits of Zemkla.

At this late date the various levels of government are still making a big joke over the UFO situation. It may turn out that each man will have to be concerned about his own understanding of the interplanetary cultural exchange--- UFO's, as it does not appear that any truth is forth-coming from the so-called "public servants". Perhaps we should give them another nineteen years to grasp the idea that this is not the only inhabited planet, or another twenty-eight years to ponder the implications of the H.G. Wells radio production of "War on The Worlds".

It is interesting to note that data has been given out to "just plain folks"; the kind of people that don't mind being called "New Agers". In this way the word is being passed along as people eat lunch together, on the job where we have worked for years side-by-side to someone who has seen one, or at a spacecraft convention. The author has spoken to many social groups and metaphysical conventions, where we as Americans can exercise the freedom of speech and talk about what we see in the skies. As citizens we have an obligation to report facts as we observe UFO's, to the proper authorities. Time, direction, number of craft, and general discription of visibility. These reports should receive consideration, but "little green men stories" have lowered the opinion that the public information officers have of the entire subject of UFO's. Perhaps the "guy on the street" is the only one qualified to handle truth after all.

The Air Force should know that a two-man spacecraft had landed and was captured by the Russian Government, and this was the basic reason for the sudden change of "UFO policy". If all, or at least some facts were known the American public would realize the government has our best interests at heart. But now, after not being informed about the various events as they have occured to suddenly be told all the facts the people would probably "run for the hills" as the government believes. The H.G. Wells account of an invasion of this earth by Martians remains in the minds of those who are with holding UFO information. Ask yourself this question: "Could the American public 'take it' if they were told the truth"?

These events were occuring at about the same time and the Air Force was making a desperate effort to try to capture a spacecraft, just to keep up with the Russians. While these frantic efforts continued the two men that the Russians captured educated the Russian scientists on rocket propulsion. No other group of people on this planet know as much as the Kiev Scientists on rocket propulsion. The material that has been given could be described as knowledge about the basic principles of the rocket engine any school boy from Selo would know about. A parallel situation would be a group of scientists being told about horse-drawn carriages as a help to build a combustion engine. The data given is so elementary that it is not of any real help to the Russian scientists. Their superior knowledge in the field of rocket propulsion has allowed the USSR to gain a valuable advantage over the USA in the "moon space race". It was because of these reasons that the members of the crew on the spacecraft were not eager to place themselves in a position where they too might be captured and trapped in the time-space quantrom of so backward a planet as the Earth.

The recent UFO "flap" following August 3rd, 1965, and the subsequent "reactions" in the Watts area are of a result to a crude device that darted back and forth across over America. The reason the military intelligence went into a panic was that it was not only the start of wide range Russian experimentation and testing of devices built from the copy of the captured disk; but also two other alarming features:

The first of these is only a matter of logical deduction, the Air Force has has quite a time trying to explain away the sighting of Keinith Arnold. However, that sighting was a "tea party" compared with 10,000 Amarican tax payers seeing the same craft dart back and forth along the same flight path for several days. The many photos and drawings published by the newspapers didn't help the Air Force in their routine de-bunking.

The second is that these sightings add to the probability that the Russians have learned how to operate the captured two-man device or Russian copies. It is clear that the USSR has developed beyond the elementary stages of rocket propulsion.

These are not minor issues and "like it or not" this will have an effect on the peoples of this 'ol Earth, regardless who believes what. In 1947 the only issue was whether or not to reveal the truth about the UFO's to the public, now it is a different story. It might be well to mention that not all governments use information or the lack of it as a tool to control "free minded citizens" to think exactly what minority decides. Bear in mind that observations of flying saucers, UFO's, or flying street lamps by the Air Force were observed long before the Air Force existed and accounts of contacts and sightings go back thousands of years. Some of which are still in the Christian Bible. Currently, UFO expert, Dr. J. Allen Hynek stated that spring thaws in Florida released trapped gases resulting resulting from decomposing organic material in the swamps have produced the object seen from Australia to Michigan in a flurry of eerie UFO sightings. Certainly we should realize the difficult time they are having trying to convince so many hundreds of people that they are only observing supersonic butterflies, wild ducks or swamp gas; when at the same time cameras, radar and American citizens are in agreement, i.e., photos of spacecraft match with what our people claim they have seen over America. The notion that our "free expression" is controled is not a happy thought. Restriction of public information with held by public servants, paid by the public taxpayer, to collect said information to be kept from the public seems strange. Now on top of everything, the combined commands have the additional problem of explaining away 10,000 citizens seeing the same UFO, plus the Air Force swallowing of egos, admitting that "we are not the only Cat Fish in the sea". Imagine the frustrations of the Air Force observing a solid craft darting back and forth across the USA at speeds beyond 42,000 miles per hour; ordering a pilot to get in a jet and chase a craft that can circle the globe before a pilot can climb into a rocket thrust-winged aircraft.

ROCKETS, RUSSIANS, AND SPACECRAFT

The latest dasterdly act to occur over our skies was the destruction of one of the spacecraft sent here originally by planet Selo and which was stationed near the surface of planet Earth. The opposing Russian experimental craft sent out from behind their curtain of silence had the nerve to travel between two planetary vortexes, which happen to connect a line roughly drawn from Boston to Los Angeles. The most common mistake that is made about spacecraft is that they are believed to be propelled by force through our atmosphere. This is not true. They, by scientific means, "overcome time and space". They do not generally move through the air from one point to another. They (from the viewpoint of a person standing on the ground, fixed at least from motion) dematerialize and rematerialize again at another point in time and space. The reason for this belief is that we tend to project our own methods of flight onto other persons not of this world.

The speculations of Dr. Albert Eienstien have a germ of fact in them concerning his ideas about relitivity and straight line flight which exceeds the speed of light. Such a body (vehicle to transport people) would pass into a different time quantrum and thus not be observable.

The two men that are being held by the Russians are just as human as the rest of us and have eager families awaiting word that they will be released and free to return home. We are all subject to "situations of entrapment", be it self-induced; like being "lost on the desert", or locked in a prison cell. The event that caused their entrapment was in October of 1959, and the many UFO policies reflect the state of confusion our top military have concerning "what to do" about the "swamp gas" traveling at supersonic speeds, while aircraft attempt to catch them.

The solar system from which these men were sent is called Wolf-4 or more popularly known as the Alpha Centuri Star. This star is the central radiating body of their home planet which has at least been detected by our telescopes. It is pathetic that we can photograph a flying saucer and not believe our eyes, or the resulting photograph. The concept that these two men were born on a planet other than our own seems to be beyond "Joe Public's" thinking ability. The disk that was captured is capable of complete materialization or dematerialization. However, without interest, concern, or belief in spiritual law, a working knowledge of how to control the device was impossible. Another reason for the shock of such a craft appearing over our skies and racing back and forth was that it appeared as if it were out of control and the pilot was frantically trying to gain control. Planet Selo is only one of seven planets in our group; including our planet, seven groups in one sector, fourty-nine in all. These seven planets are linked together by a spiritual bond of understanding as well as Karmic help in the form of a desire for cultural exchange. Our planet Earth is the only one in our sector of space at the time of this writting that has not been invited to be part of TABOF. Interplanetary exchange has allowed the others to share their vast scientific knowledge. The other six planets of which Selo is the closest, not only in distance and scientific development, but Zemkla was given the same assignment which in our time reference was February 5, 1962. Yet they have already completed so much that they can partake of the wealth of knowledge of the other five planets which are more advanced. A great deal of information of an advanced nature has been given to our planet, but there are very few that have been trained to receive and apply this knowledge. The book call "Gateway" is an example of this as the entire body of research data presently offered by the "Institute of Parapsychology" is their complete method of personal training. At this point the reader might expect a description of these methods; however, that is not the purpose of this writing.* The course that the Institute of Parapsychology was entrusted with by the "Space Brothers" was given with the intention that it would be given out to all who are sincere seekers of truth.

RUSSIAN FLAP "65"

There are two very reasonable Russian achievements to date: First, the USSR scientists have the best and most advanced knowledge concerning rocketry and related subjects, and secondly, the disk has been dismantled and duplicated.

The first area would contain information that would have been useful to all mankind if it had been released to the world. As to the spacecraft, each part has been copied and as recent as April of 1961, the USA learned that the Russian Government had successfully duplicated a craft.* It is important that the reader try to grasp the military signifance and the reaction that Stratigic Air Command might have when such a craft appears over America and proceeds to display superior tactical manuvers. The origional five craft that were assigned to this planet have now been reduced to one. The craft were deployed as follows: one in Kiev , two which returned to their home base on Selo, one shot down by the Russian device, and the one remaining spacecraft operated by Zemkla.

The fact that the Russians have the ability to put the captured device into the air no one can doubt; the question is, can they do so without wrecking it or

---

*Although the craft has been duplicated the principles of drive have not, nor have they been understood by the Russian scientists as of this printing,(1966).

*For details on how to enroll in this course through the mail or in person, write: Institute of Parapsychology, c/o Galaxy Press. Ask for free booklet and schedule of classes.

killing the pilot? So many people have seen the "bell-shaped craft" that not only are people in the field familar with them, but even toy manufacturers have adapted the design. The photographs and drawings of the "thing" flying back and forth over America does not even begin to resemble a saucer. It appeared more like a crude assemblage of some small boys making a make-believe car out of apple boxes. Yet we are forced to admit it was there. It did fly and it was effective in terms of military destruction. The flight path also tells us that the Russians have learned about the six planetary vortexes, as the device was guided back and forth along the line of force between two major vortexes.

Every human invention with controls is subject to human error, regardless how perfect that device might have been built. Although the Russians captured a fantastic device this does not imply that they have the ability or understanding to operate it. Now about seven years later it would seem reasonable to assume that they would know a little more about it and the possibility that they have attempted flights is not unreasonable.

ALZURA, SATIN'S DOMAIN

The force of light as it expands with consciousness pushes back a front of darkness. At the same time it must gradually overcome spiritual darkness as men and women develop their inner spiritual heritage. While we generally only think and speak in a positive manner we must not act as the ostrich and stick our heads in the sand in order to "not see evil". While the planet Selo and five other have overcome the Alzur forces on their planets and have thus entered into what has been called the "Golden Age" or the Ultimate Civilization; some have lost the battle to the dark forces. In space there are many planets that have tried to overcome the forces of darkness but failed and fell under their control. Through this method Alzdom has gained complete control not only of the human bodies from those planets but any and all physical means of transportation of that planet. These animated human bodies look like normal humans yet are not of the spiritual race of God. On the physical level they conduct their affairs with one goal in mind, overcoming new planets and thus providing instrumentation for their kind, or in plain language bodies.

They have about the same feeling about their project as people do that are working on a political campaign. That is they have hopes that their side will win and believe their system is the best. Their chief weapon aside from the obvious one, FEAR is that almost all peoples tend to sit around and DO NOTHING UNTIL IT IS TOO LATE! When their activities become too obvious then they simply remove those persons that learn too much; however, there is no great concern as the general public will not heed warning and tend to laugh at these ideas.

Most New Age students of Light, Life, and Love know this activity as one of two words: (1) Possession or (2) Obsession. Through these two methods it is possible to gain control of one human body through which very effective work can be accomplished.

The principles of the Indole as described in the book, "The Indole, Microcosm of Man"*, shows that by certain methods released by TABOF into the custody of the Institute of Parapsychology it is possible to purify the body and spiritualize it. Applying the basic concepts of logic it would be clear (although details will not be described at this time) that whatever the process or method, it most certainly could be reversed. If for example one stops eating pork to clean out the system, then eating great amounts of pork would be a method of helping the forces of darkness to take over and control the person that eats this Indole Poison.

The very first step in spiritual development is the control of your biology through care of the physical body. Cleansing the body and getting on a proper diet must be done before anything along the lines of spiritual development can be done. There is a general belief among student of truth that there is a connection between alcohol and possessions. This is true, as alcohol is a indole poison.

Aside from the microcosmic war that is taking place within the human structure, there are those who have come from the outer darkness of space, that have fallen into the Alzur control. In our review of this aspect of the "Spacecraft Story" it is our attempt to stick to the warfare between solid craft in the sky as this is all that the general public is interested in hearing about.

---

*"The Indole, Microcosm of Man", available through the Institute of **Parapsychology**.

THE SPIRITUAL BEING

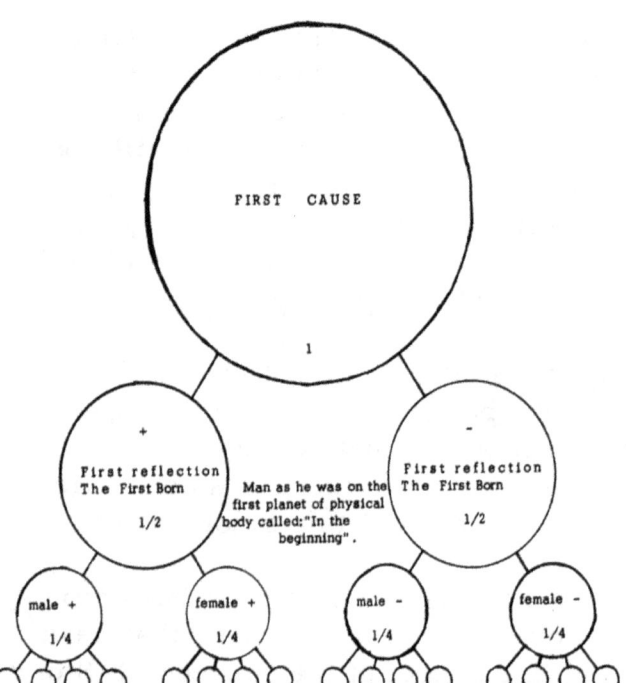

Man as he was on the first planet of physical body called: "In the beginning".

On planet earth about 1/2 billion souls have now lowered themselves another full octive. Within these only 1/16th of their God-self remains. Although the author was not allowed to speak concerning methods people of earth use to lower their vibration and serve the Prince of Darkness, it now becomes necessary to indicate that at least 1/6th of the people of earth serve Satan.

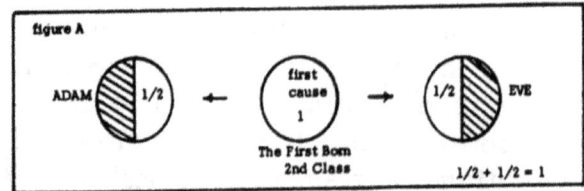

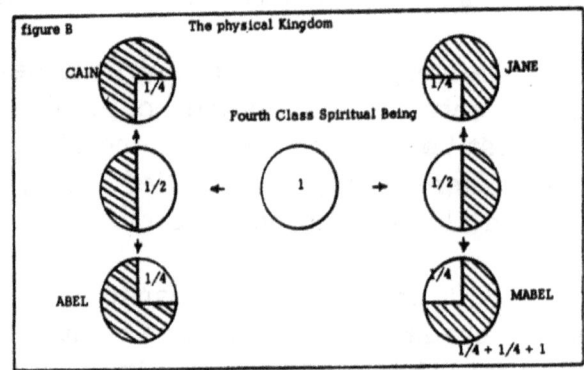

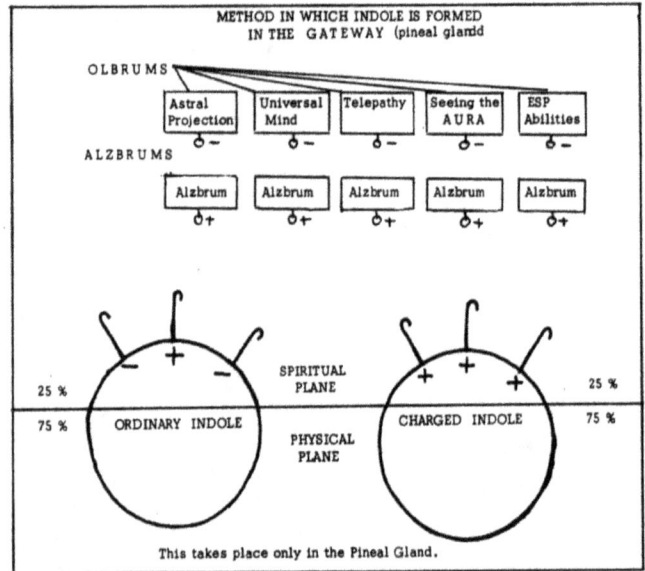

Each indole must attach to three different objects on the spiritual plane before it can be effective. Ordinary Indoles have one positive hook and two negative hook. Since all Olbrums have negative hoops they can only unite with the one positive hook on the ordinary Indole. To achieve fany degree of Superconsciousness the indoles must be increased to such an extent as will make up for the two negative hooks on each ordinary indole. Three Indoles will attract three Olbrums. One charged Indole will attract three Olbrums. Charged indoles result from use of the "Method" and proper diet in conjunction with the proper use of Shel. An increase in ordinary Indoles is necessary to allow the "one hook, ordinary indole" to attract enough Olbrums to cause any psychic effects. In the spiritual realm, all objects are negatively charged except Alzbrums. Alzbrums are attracted to the negative hooks of the ordinary indoles. Alzbrums cause a dulling of all of the physical sences, the brain and of psychic abilities. There is a ratio of 1 Alzbrum to 10,000 Olbrums; however less than 1% of the spiritual being which is composed of Olbrums is within the physical body. This seems slight but remember that on the ordinary indole there are two negative hooks to the one positive hook. The positive Alzbrum is drawn to the indole because of the negative and positive attraction, even through there are 10,000 Olbrums for each Alzbrum.

Our objective is twofold: Either create all charged indoles or increase the number of ordinary INDOLES. Charged indoles can only be created when the body is in perfect shape through perfect diet and exercise, plus the Shel. Alzbrums are created by incorrect diet. Correct diet destroys Alzbrums; effect of Shel is to create charged indoles.

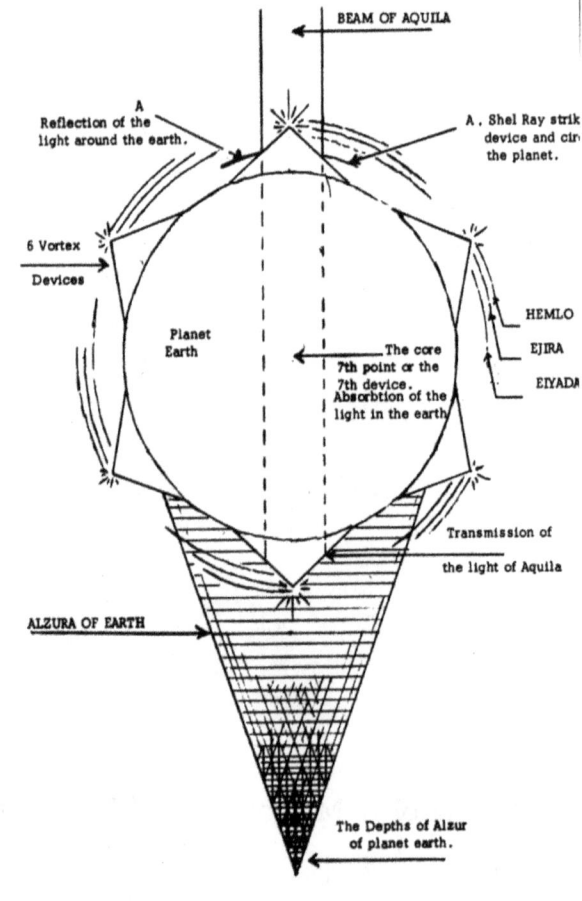

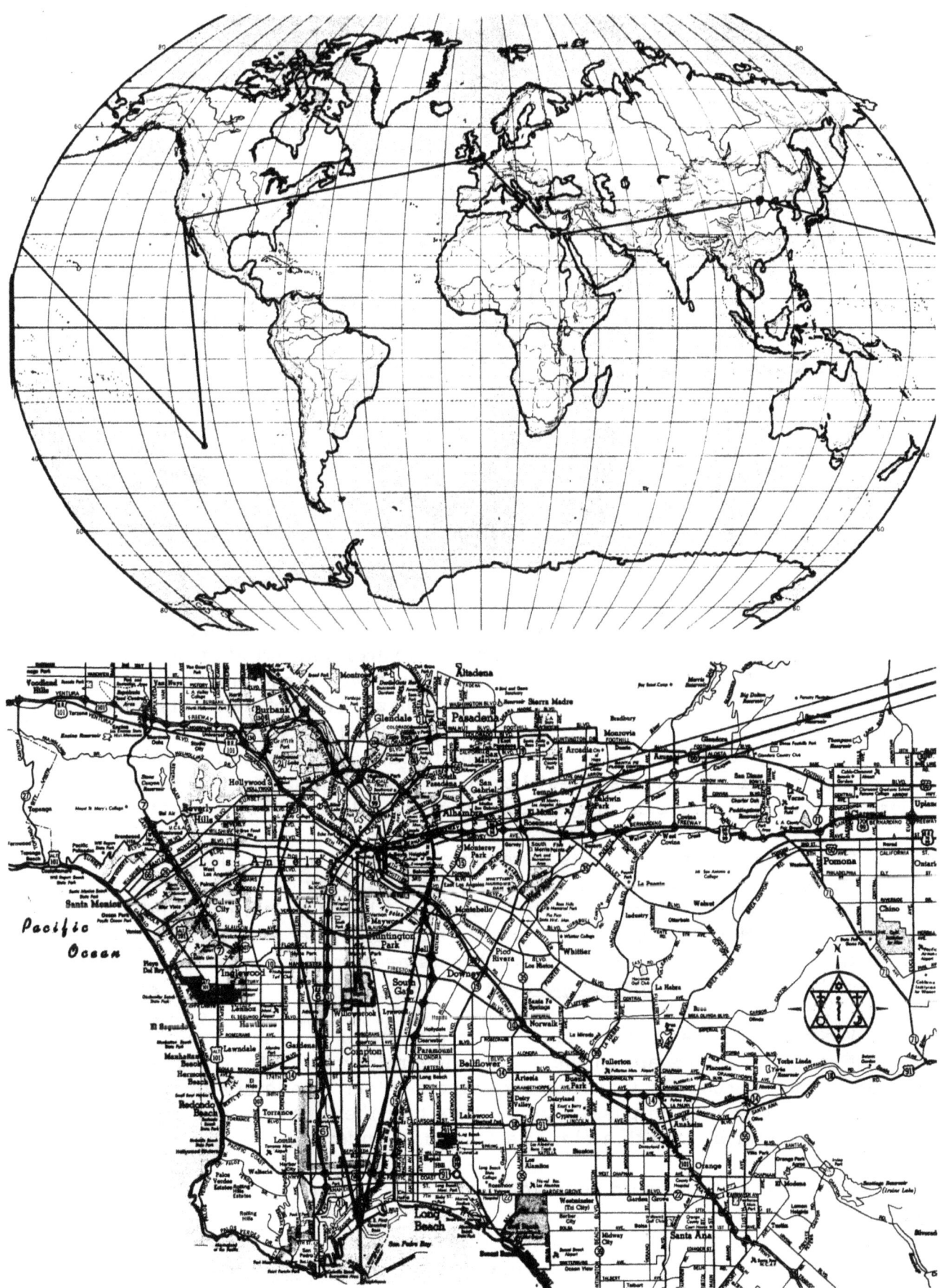

24

REIGN of FAHSZ

To grasp the full meaning of the Commandments as given to the "Church of The Universe" something should be known about the basic government for all of the universe, known as "God's Law". It created such that each sector has seven groups of planets, seven planets in each group, 49 planets in all. Spiritual beings as created by the One Father were originally equal and had free will and choice. A master by the name of Fahsz is the Sector Commander, of which planet Earth is part--a very small part. It is his spiritual assignment to receive the word through his direct superior, Master Brrrsgv and pass this on the fourty-nine planetary avatars, who are responsible to instrument it on their respectible planets.

Starting from the top there is "The One Father", and around him seven cardinal virtues or precepts. One of which is Brrrsgv. He has around him "Seven Masters", one of which is Fahsz. Fahsz has control and jurisdiction of this sector of space. "The Council of Seven Planets" is seven planetary Avatars; seven of these groups, 49 in all, form the Council of Fahsz. Each of these planetary Avatars is the spokesmen in tangible form of the spiritual consciousness of each planet. In all, seven groups of seven planets each of fourty-nine inhabited member planets. This does not suggest however, that all planets are inhabited or that there are only 49 planets in this sector out of the billions of solar systems.

The specific commandments have varied for each age as they are to be interwoven into the existing culture, so as to seem as if they came from a religious group on each planet. People in this "New Age" should be able to handle the fact that this is not the only inhabited planet in existence, nor the most advanced. It is for this reason that the same commandments as before are given but <u>without any attempt to conceal their source, purpose, or causation.</u>

We on Heros (Earth) are one of seven planets of the same group--"Group VII". Not all of these planets are on the same structural cycle. We on this earth are of course of the "Carbon Cycle"; however, others in our "planetary seven" are of the "Phosphorous Cycle". In passing, take note that there are many other cycles not mentioned and far beyond this planet's scientific understanding at the present.

While all of this would seem to be strictly a metaphysical or an occult activity, this is not true. By use of extended sensory abilities some of our citizens can now see beyond the range of others. Metaphysical? No, they might on a ship at sea use a telescope which can enlarge an object. Others still using only their eyesight can be taught to see objects on the sea prior to those with a physical device. Our growth as a civilization is twofold: First physical scientific advances and secondly sensory development, i.e., extra sensory perception.

It may very well be that when history looks back on our actions they will all be seen as cultural and social advancements, not occult activities. Just as our medical, mathematical, and chemical sciences were considered as "way out" in their introduction, and now are accepted, so will our acts be judged. These will be seen simply as cultural advancements attained because we will eventually gain interplanetary contact and the influx of the methodologies from advanced civilzations will come to our planetary shores. This is really no more fantastic than the start of international commerce and steam ships.

CREATION*

In the begining, which was never, the Divine Father dwelt in his circle and the circles seven points. With Him was Alzur, the Prince of Darkness. The Divine Father in creating existence made one evil, one good for each evil. He cast Alzur out of Heaven. Alzur into eternal darkness, the Anti-Universe. For each good, the Father created its opposite number in Alzur, bad for good. The Divine Father has a plan whereby good will over come bad bit by bit, piece by piece. The Divine Father decided he whould develop places for souls to live. He sent the Force of Shel coupled with the Force of Hal forming the Indole. This the Divine Father did in His own spiritual likeness. All is either in the likeness of the Divine Father or like Alzur, and not necessarily in a human form.

PLANETARY AVATARS

The One Father has around him a circle and on part of that circle is Master Brrrsgv. Brrrsgv has around him a circle and on part of this circle is Master Fahsz. Master Fahsa is in complete charge of this sector of space and within it is one part of that circle called Anahsz. The consciousness called Anahsz represents the developing consciousness of this planet Earth. When this Earth comes into its own it will manifest the leading qualities for six other planets, not of this solar system. This group, "The Planetary Seven", is part of a larger group. The total group is known as TABOF. It consists of 49 planets in all of which Master Fahsz is in charge.

---

* From the "Books of Fahsz", volume I, chapter intittled Creation.

THE FATHER'S COMMANDMENTS *

1. There is One Father, everlasting.

2. The One Father is supreme; knowledge and light, worship no other.

3. The Divine Father commands that you will not kill.

4. The Divine Father commands you will not steal.

5. The Divine Father commands you will not pervert light.

6. The Divine Father commands you will meditate.

7. The Divine Father commands you nourish the body.

8. The Divine Father commands you do only those things to other persons that you would want them to do to you.

9. The Divine Father commands that you be aware.

10. The Divine Father commands that you do good, weighing all the circumstances, and do the best in regards to all bearing in mind that it might bring harm to others.

11. The Divine Father commands that you be peaceful.

12. The Divine Father commands that you observe time.

These twelve basic rules of conduct are universal for all levels of human life in all of the various sectors of space. Those planets which have fallen "out of the light" have become part of the forces of darkness and MUST always try to confuse and pervert the truth. On the side of Light, the good and the righteous are the Brothers of The Light, The Great White Brotherhood, Brothers of The Illuminati, and The Masters. This scant number is but a few; all future referances of those that do the work of the "One Father" and keep His word will be referred to as TABOF. Make a very clear distinction in your own mind that there are two groups. Alzur and Good, because your life and spiritual development may very well depend on your knowing the difference.

* See "The Twelve Commandments Explained", a book on interpretation of The Twelve Commandments.

UNIVERSAL LAW

The basis for everything is the First Cause, the One Father, Spiritual Law, and Order. To attempt to explain all of this to the average "guy on the street", who has no background in spiritual values or is not a "New Ager" would be pointless. For he could not grasp the vast significance of the Planetary Seven. To him reincarnation, karma, and UFO's are just a lot of huey! What will have to be done is to put our books in order so that our position as a member planet in the Planetary Seven, as well as the entire sector, can be brought about in a gradual manner. The only reason that these interplanetary contacts are of concern to the military is politically they have projected their own ideas into the intent of the "Space Brothers". They can only think in terms of bombs, bullets, atomic warheads, and that their budget is provided for to defend our country from attack by flying saucers. We cannot expect our war chiefs to be very good ambassadors of good will between this and another planet.

There have been so many behind-locked-door conferances on the subject of flying saucers that even the clergy have good reason to be concerned. An ever increasing number of good church members are seeing UFO's and are worried as to if observing one constitutes a "sin". In several ministerial meetings over the past years the author has heard testimony to the effect that various people have burned photographs when a spacecraft happened to be on the film. Thus they hope to remain "good christians" by distroying the evidence that UFO's exist. There is nothing in the Christian Bible that speaks against UFO's. Quite the contrary, many sections of the Bible mention them. As with the Air Force, the main problem is too many people are looking up and seeing what is physically there; and this adds to the "cover-up" problem.

Perhaps the general public does not realize it but there are meetings taking place on many different levels such as the clergy, during which they are told the truth concerning the saucers and how to keep the people from panicking. Recently, during one of these meetings, some 200 color slides of government and private photographs were shown; and the various ministers told some of the situations that had occured in their church. In most cases the person seeing the spacecraft felt guilty about having such an experience. There was implication that perhaps they were not being good citizens or christians by reason of seeing or photographing objects in the sky.

The entire situation has become so critical that it appears that we as a civilization are between tow decisions similar to that of the Air Force. The first, go through all of our data, item per item, correcting things as we go through at least 6,250 years of history. Secondly, try to adjust and make solid interplanetary contacts; and deal with the "correct and absolute facts" from here on in. These are contained in the planetary groups of TABOF. It is their purpose to give to this planet a complete library containing all knowledge. The only catch is that we have to first show a degree of regard for our fellow man, live the Golden Rule, and put our minds to work at making this a better place to live. This means to stop developing new and better ways of killing each other.

THE CHURCH OF THE UNIVERSE

The Church of The Universe includes teachings from all of the planets and all of the areas of space where the human race is in existance. The human race pervades the universe; however, in some cases they may not look human by our concepts. The important point is that all who have a human soul are of the human race. Having a soul is the one fact that distinguishes the human race in all areas. The Church of The Universe has been founded on the 9th Inner Circle. Here the teachings are the very highest and the plan for perfect sharing and perfect love radiated to all parts of the universe.

The most fundamental truth is that God, the Creator, is part of every aspect of His creation. Everything in the universe is God, of God, and God.

The Church of The Universe builds pyramids on each planet inhabited by the human soul, or the "spiritual being" located on the six planetary vortexes. There will come and Avatar to this planet and there shall be peace on the Earth: those who do not follow him shall commence the redevelopment of their souls from the <u>lowest plane of existence</u>. They shall go through many millions of incarnations before they shall be given another chance to enter the Kingdom as described in the book, "Going Up!". The gate to the Kingdom has the appearance of the eye of a needle. Very few can pass through the eye of the needle, and only through the force of Anahsz may this occur.

The purpose of the Church of The Universe is the development of all human souls to prepare themselves for their life in the Kingdom. TABOF is dedicated to rid the planet Earth of all Alzur force in what ever form it might manifest it self.

FAHSZ

Fahsz was created by the One Father as the supreme and divine messenger of "The Kingdom of God" to this sector of space, and bearer of all knowledge of the One Father. Fahsz is the only true messenger.

Fahsz lowered his vibration such that all the people of this planet Earth could see his physical form. Fahsz said unto the people of Earth: "All shall be **given** the means that they may enter the Kingdom of God, whosoever believes on **me and** accepts the coming of Anahsz as taught by your priests. These shall dwell eternally in the Kingdom of God".

The people of Earth who were assembled for this occasion sent great laughter at Fahsz and Fahsz left planet Earth saying, "I am but a shadow, never more shall mortal men look upon the face of Fahsz". This directive has been carried out through the ages and no man (of this planet Earth) has seen Fahsz directly.

THE CHARTS of FAHSZ

FAHSZ As time turns 250,000 years		
	Period I 62,500 years	The 2,500 years of Abraham 60,000 years
	Period II 62,000 years	12,500 years ATLANTIS 50,000 years required for Atlantis to become The city of God. The prosperous period of Atlantis. FAHSZ appeared 50,000 years Lemuria - Stonehenge Vortex Device Atlantis sinks TABOF ordered Nui to build time capsule
	Period III 62,500 years	Lemuria, last to sink The Father put a full end to all perversions. Nui and the Flood 12,500 years. People begin to inhabit the earth again. ANTILA The first appearance of Anahsz.
	Period IV 62,500 years	27 years in building the Great Spiritual Temple The Vortex device in Egypt, Gizeh. ALL people of the earth gathered at the Egypt Pyramid to take part in the activation ceremonies of the Device. "The Two", agents of Alzur gained control of the people and brought about the entombment of the Avatar and the Pyramid builders. The Avatar used the Vortex Device and returned to ANTILA. He destroyed the Pyramid of Fahsz, returned the Akashic records to the "Time Capsule of Nui" and stopped the earth. When the earth turned again, memory was smitten from every mind. A new kingdom was set up called Egypt, led by the great prophet Neffertiti who was honored in the kingdom. Antila became Egypt.
	The New Age	Feb. 5th, 1962 Great planetary conjunction Sign of Fahsz. Completion of the mission - all of the 144,000 shall remove the Alzur force from their bodies - with the Vortex devices from planet earth - in combined work from our group of seven planets - and from this part of space, including all fourth-nine graduating planets.

Indirect communication has been constantly in operation on this planet as each Avatar in his turn attempts to complete the holy mission of the One Father. For this reason there is a selection by personal effort to wear the crown of Avatar. The history and knowledge of Fahsz, including the Akashic Records of Earth, are to be passed along as each attempts to complete the assignment.

Fahsz now dwells in the Kingdom of God and shall not appear again until an Avatar of Earth has completed the earthly work, at which time there shall be a congreation of the Great Multitudes of the Kingdom. The Great White Brotherhood, TABOF, and all of the holy beings of the Universe shall meet at the planet Earth and shall celebrate the deliverance of the souls of this planet Anahsz. At this time Fahsz shall again appear to men, and wipe away the shadwo, sending it forever into Alzur.

All the knowledge that is needed is given to all men of all ages. There is no living being on the face of this Earth that is outside the love of the One and only Father. We are all children of the one Parent. Races and structural differences are but the result of the dividing of the Universal race of man into its component parts, and climatic conditions man consciously forces upon his body.

Fahsz is to the other planets in our group of seven referred to as "Sector Commander", for they see him as a physical being. In this "New Age" Fahsz has directed spacecraft, flying saucers or interplanetary vehicles to make contact with the "people" of this planet. Only five senses are active for those who are now on this planet, thus Fahsz, through TABOF and the Interplanetary Council must appeal through the five senses to the people of Earth.

ANAHSZ

The history of man on this planet abounds with Eastern and esoteric philosophies and in this "New Age" souls seek the hidden truth of God. There will come a time when each person will be classified as with the One Father or against Him. Those who serve and keep the first commandment as given to Moses an Avatar, "to love thy God, with all thy heart, and all thy soul" will be risen as those of Alzdom die in the holocaust.

At the proper time Anahsz as he was known to Isaiah shall emerge and lead this entire world to the heavenly wonder and awe of the Kingdom of the One Father.

The birth of Anahsz occured 25,000 years prior to February 5, 1962. This was not a birth of a physical woman. Anahsz stepped from the Kingdom of the One Father as a spiritual being to this earthly planet as an adult male. This started the "Four Cycles of Anahsz". This all started the days the Earth stood still. This is recorded in our Bible and the ancient Chinese history; however, the exact date was February 5, 1962. Anahsz stepped onto this plane through the River of Life. This was so startling to the people that this method has never been repeated.

Only the last of the "Four Cycles of Anahsz" have been recorded in our current history books. During which there were four major leaders: Nefertiti, Isaish, Jesus, and Anahsz. It is proper and fitting that the people of this planet hold the name of Jesus in the highest as he remains the figure-head of the Avatar of Earth at this time.

Anahsz who has come to this planet three times in a male body, entered embodiment in 1935. Knowledge of him is known to but a few including the "High Priest of Tibet".

Of the small portion of history that has escaped the censoring pen of Alzdom, there remains very little evidence of the handy work of Anahsz, champion of "truth" on the Earth. Knowing that this Earth would be the last to develop, the right arm of Fahsz has been placed on this last school of the "sector of Fahsz".

While special work is being done by TABOF through the Inner Planes and the interplanetary devices parade back and forth over a deaf and dumb world special instructions have been graciously given to the author of this book. These have been given so that those who wish may remove the Alzbrums from their bodies and receive personal instructions. Those choosing to serve Satan and Alzdom will purge each other from the face of this earth and make Watts seem as a tea party. The methods given in this systematic coarse of instructions seem amazingly simple when first read, however progressively bitter to the belly and stuborn mind.

MESSAGE from SPACE

As an attempt to understand what will come to pass on this planet, during an interview with Zemkla, I asked for his description of the events that led up to the establishment of the Laws of the One Father on planet Selo, which are referred to in the "Books of Fahsz", as well as the Christian Bible.

On February 5, 1962, Earth time, the will of the One Father descended upon Zemkla: a citizen of Selo, 3rd planet from the Alpha Centuri Star.

At that time there existed on Selo a remarkably advanced civilization, and among its wonders was a device mentioned which could be called the "home news". With the daily events being presented in each home as they take place the story of Zemkla and his investigations were known almost immediately. Many on that planet had for some time followed his progress so when he received word about the mission he requested all people that were serious about carrying out the wishes of the One Father to gather on an uninhabited continent.

Zemkla led the group to that continent and eventually had what we might call the "cream of the spiritual crop" located at one point on planet Selo. He then directed a city be built to house a greater number and continued to attract large multitudes into this city. When all was in working order he taught them about the Planetary Seven, of the effort on Prismov by Temkla, the next higher planet, as well as the success of the other four planets. With a strong hand he taught the serious minded people and together they removed the Alzur from the people, their homes, cities, and finally their planet.

Once this was accomplished all efforts were directed to teach the One Father's word and build the first Pyramid of Fahsz. This temple was completed October of 1964 (Earth time). It was at this time that I was allowed the privilege of visiting their planet and seeing the Great Pyramid of Fahsz and witnessing its spiritual power. At that time only fourty million people were working on the project under the direction of Zemkla.

Zemkla was quite proud of their many accomplishments. He told me that they hoped to have another pyramid completed by Christmas of that same year, and be able to increase their members by removing the Alzur forces from the planet. I was told that the planetary Avatar on the next planet higher than Selo was Temkla. Zemkla told me that the electronic and ultra spiritual powers of Temkla far surpassed anything known to his planet. The information on how to build the pyramid and carry out the mission was greatly helped by Temkla. It seems that Temkla and a crew from their planet Prismov came with blueprints and helped Zemkla start the project. In the same manner those above Temkla had visited his planet and helped him.

As I heard of the events that led to the construction of the first Pyramid of Fahsz on planet Selo, I began to share their happiness for accomplishing so much. It was clearly explained to me that each of the planets must help those lower than themselves. As yet there has been very little communication between the first six groups of seven planets due to the necessity for all of the planets in each of seven groups to complete the work and erect the Pyramids of Fahsz. Having done all of these things Planet Selo and Prismov shared the knowledge given to them by the other planets who had already completed the project.

INSIDE THE CRAFT

Again I heard the signal and understood that I should drive out to the place where I had met Zemkla so many times before. Although I have done this often, the same thrill of wonder fills my mind with speculation as to what might take place. When the craft appeared it looked like a star or a very small sun which grew in brilliance. I felt rooted to the spot, not daring to look away. A moment later it landed and I hurried across the clearing anticipating the opening of a door. As I waited my eyes scanned the surface of the craft and I found myself speculating and searching for the location of the door. When the electronic pulsation, which was not very loud, stopped, the door appeared.

I had been cautioned earlier not to touch the craft until "the device" had been turned off and the craft would be at rest. When I was first given this caution my first thought was to avoid the danger of some form of radiation. My mind was soon put at ease when it was explained that coming into contact with the craft would re-arrange my molecular structure. I was to understand this only years later when the driving method was explained to me in clear detail.

As the door opened I saw Zemkla step out (we had become friends after many meet-tings), and take several strides away from the craft. Generally speaking this had always been the point when the door would close behind him and the craft would dart back into the sky. To my surprise it did not move but remained. I could only hope that my wildest dream would come true. Would this by my chance to visit and see first hand the inside of the craft? My imagination did flips; wanting so much and yet time after time being turned down, I did not have the heart to ask again. I was completely surprised when Zemkla invited me aboard. I felt no hesitation. Quickly I stepped on the ramp and grasped the rail with my right hand. I felt a slight tingling sensation run through my body as the craft neutralized my body charge. I wondered whether the craft was a thinking thing and perhaps some sort of feelings about my presence there. I was told that most of these things were handled by the various computers located on the craft. All forms that use the principles of light have a relationship with life, thus the strange aura and thought patterns.

I was greeted by a light that was of a pulsating **green**. It caused everything to look strange and foreboding. After the initial shock I accepted the new spectrum it produced without giving it another thought.

The crew did not exchange words, but looked at me in a strange manner. Looking back, I must have stared at them too. After all, I looked as unusual to them as they did to me. They looked similar to Zemkla in appearance: like so many professional athletes and models. They wore a one piece form-fitting uniform which was accented by one marking--the "Seal of Fahsz". It was worn on their left shoulder. A heavy chain hung around their neck; on it was the "Seal of Fahsz". It seemed to be some sort of device. It was important that each person on the craft be tuned on a specific vibratory wave length, or have the molecular "sameness" as the craft.

The craft was divided into three sections: each had a doorway much like a submarine bulkhead located between each section. This craft was equipped with one third section devoted to scientific recording devices on which the activities were then recorded on strips of paper. Once in the craft the door was sealed, all I could hear was a humming sound deep within the floor. It was explained to me that should a single jet aircraft be dispatched to our area the craft would have to ascend beyond pursuit range instantly to avoid attack. While on the craft all were subject to the operational orders of the Captain in charge and on several occasions I have found myself seperated from my car. Freedom of movement within the craft is restricted when the craft is in a danger area such as the Earth. When in space or on their planet they were eager to show me through every part , opening lockers to display planetary equipment.

The major portion of the craft was below our feet, yet not anywhere was there a sound beyond the hum that filled the cabin. Certain of the mechanical activity was directed up the "centerpost" which conveys the power to a ball-like shape on the housing. The controls were set in a panel some 16 feet along the wall and a single operator controled these by remaining in a uni-rail seat that traveled the full scope of the control panel. The panel looked very much like that back stage in a theater with a great many levers of bright colors. Although one of the most thrilling experiences of my life it always produces a feeling of awe for the electrical know-how built into the flying saucer.

Discussion about their craft and the application of spiritual law to physical instrumentation was discussed in great detail. It seems that once mankind, for any planet stops; thinking of using God-given force for selfish gains and applies them spiritually, he will grow up. This yields not only interplanetary transportation, but development in the areas of social, religion, and science, thus, being helped by other advanced planets. This is the pattern that the One Father wishes to be followed. By carrying out his wishes there will be progress; going contrary to the will of the One Father we of the Planet Hiros will remain in our present backward state. Following the will of the flesh or the forces of Alzur is contrary to God's law.

I have found that by tape recording these instruction and conversations it is very

The excitement of seeing so many things caused specific details to blur in my mind and it was not until I had the privilege of several visits that I settled down to looking at one thing at a time. While at first all I wanted was to travel in a spacecraft. I soon learned that there was a certain stigma about it. Firstly, I no more than left the craft and started home in my car when a feeling of frustration came over me. Here I was in a new car traveling at top speed on the freeway, which is just about the ultimate in transportation on planet Earth, when just a few minutes before I was in a spacecraft traveling at speeds beyond my own understanding and seeing common surface craft traveling automatically at great speeds. It forced me to change my way of thinking to see so many wonderful devices on planet Selo. After many months of these experiences I began to appreciate what was being done for me in relative proportion. When Zemkla and his co-workers came in for a talk my attitude of acceptance allowed for a greater amount of accomplishment. They too seemed to realize that the original excitement became under control and they were able to explain many more thrilling facts to me about the interplanetary contact.

At the very end of the visit I was sorry to leave and return to so backward a civilization; however as Zemkla pointed out this condition would quickly change when communication started. In the months that followed I heard of their progress by repeated visits with Zemkla. Through these contacts it was soon apparent that they had completed their project by Janurary of 1964, our time. It was Zemkla's wish that I write of the things I've seen, marveled at, and been told about, to prepare the way for the coming of Anahsz.

TRIP TO SELO

Subsiquent to several encounters with Zemkla I was invited to his planet and I had the presence of mind to ask if I could take my tape recorder with me. This I was granted and we went in my car out of the city to a spot well within the planetary vortex.

The Planetary vortexes are: (1) Los Angeles, (2) Easter Island, Chile, (3) Tenri City, Japan, (4) Peking, China, (5) Gizeh, Egypt, (6) Stonehinge, England. Each vortex has a positive field of force extending "upstream" from the spot and a negative Alzur force "downstream". The detail of this can be seen on map B. The Shel's Rays: Eiyatas, Eijira & Hemlo, sweep the planet from right to left as the Earth turns. The positive position is where the Sun is directly over head and the negative spot is on the opposite side. Although I had deduced the general location of the six planetary vortexes of planet Earth, I did not know exactly why the cpacecraft selected a certain place to land. Zemkla tried to explain that although I did not realize it at the time, the area where I had gone so many times to find a place to meditate was one of these vortexes. I had thought that they had picked that spot due to my many hours of meditation there; however, I was told that they paid respect to each of these vortexes even though the people in this "New Age" have not discovered the importance of them.

As we drove out from the city I tried to make conversation and asked, "what sort of freeways do you have on Selo"? Zemkla said that some day he would take me through a place where surface craft were built; however, the passage ways were similar to ours, but controled by light, the lower physical aspect of which we know as electricity. The devices are smaller and almost entirely given over to a place to sit in comfort around a small table on swivel chairs, that allow for 360 degree vision. These surface craft are guided from storage places to the pathway by consciously controlling the device from within up what we would call the "on ramp". Once on the pathway, control was semi-automatic on the outer most lanes. The center lanes which are stacked one over the other, are controled by light computers until the device is to take their "off ramp". Collisions were avoided by automatic speed controls built into the craft to adjust to other solid objects such as cars in front or back. The surface car never touches the ground except when at rest in storage, but hovers above the surface on a cushion of air. This allows for a very smooth ride. Zemkla expressed his concern for our Safety, living on a planet that allowed for such a hazardous manner of travel.

Soon we reached the place where the spacecraft was hidden and there we boarded Zemkla's personal craft. I was so wrapped up in looking at the various instrumentations that I was not aware that we had in fact left the Earth's gravity and were well out in space. The first time that I was aware of this was when I saw the view panel display the Earth as a green hued spheriod. I reflected afterwards as to if I really saw green or if I expected to see green. The major surprise was the similarity to seeing the moon. The rest of the heavens was as beautiful as it is in the desert. The faint lighting within the craft added to the thrilling experience of it all. The only sound besides the drone of the guidance system , was the whirring of the single track control chair that moved back and forth in front of a panel that covered one third of the wall surface in the craft.

I did not look out again during the 30 minute flight as I was shown throughout the saucer. The amount of moving parts and storage space really surprised me. I had thought the machine would be almost all electrical machinery, but instead the greater part was passenger space had the appearance of a cockpit in an airliner. I was told that most of the electrical operations were in the single curved wall that formed the sides of the single cabin. I had expected to find all manner of electrical devices, but after inspecting the lower level and the storage compartments I realized that the motive power was a far simpler principle that one might guess.

It would appear that we tend to project our faults and beliefs onto those of other planets, even through we have never met them on a large scale social level.

Members of their society are seen as so many "bad guys" that are constantly "trying to rustle the rancher's cattle". This truism is indicative of the emotional and egotistical state of this planet. "We are not alone", says Dr. Harlow Shapley, famed Harvard University astronomer, "for probably there are 100,000,000 planets which could support life in a high form". Despite a degree of scientific stability the American public is still maintained at the six grade level. The type of thing brought about by the radio program of H.G Wells, "War of The World", and the subsiquent "run to the hills". Under the circumstances, those in command might well wonder what might happen if they openly admitted that there is any truth behind the many thousands of photographs, radar blips, and other sundry sightings.

As the gap between Selo and the craft grew smaller I thought I could detect a feeling of eagerness among the crew that I stayed at a respectful distance. I wondered at this and tried to speculate as to what they might be thinking. The only clue was the general feeling that people of Earth were decidedly unstable. Again I noticed the Seal of Fahsz on the landing strip and I made an effort to look 360 degrees around the area prior to descending to ground zero.

The landing field, if you want to call it that, appeared more like a checker-board with craft coming and going at intervals, was directly in front of our flight path. The unusual thing was that we moved along straight lines or gradual arcs without any gradual descent or banking as in an airplane. Once over the proper checker-spot we descended and then stepped onto a type of elevator that lowered us to the ground in a leisurely manner. Being aboard an UFO while they were avoiding visual contact with jet aircraft reminded the author of the alert feeling of "crash-dive drills of World War II". It is very apparent that the experiences they have had on this planet have not been altogether pleasant.

From the craft we moved between rows of other craft to what seemed to be an elevator which took Zemkla and myself into and up inside the Pyramid of Fahsz. I asked if this was the same pyramid that I had been to visit in October of 1964, and his response was "yes". The first pyramid to be constructed on Selo was also the central base of operations on the entire planet.

We stopped our ascent inside the pyramid on a floor that is in reality a balcony just under the huge dome: like a hemisphere that forms the main hall, in which the Church of The Universe holds their services. In this great temple a stillness can be heard. Some call it the music of the spheres; but in reality the shape of the pyramid is the true cause, as structually it imitates the life form. Thus, it is quite easy to become attuned with the ALL.

After a short walk around the curved balcony we again came to a door which is of plobium, a building material that lends itself to conform with mental control. We ascended to a level where there was much activity in a large square room. By standing near to the outside wall it was easy to look out and realize that this floor was at the top of the pyramid. From a structural standpoint this also was noticable as less area was devoted to the huge columns that were seen on the lower levels. It was in this laboratory that I first learned of my mistake in the choice of tape recorder for I brought an A.C. powered recorder that had been brought there from so primitive a culture that still used poles and wires to convey their electrical energy. In a few minutes they had duplicated the necessary current to operate the recorder and Zemkla described the operations sections of the pyramid.

The over-all description seemed to be more of a bee-hive than a pyramid. The major effect however, was similar to the massive temples of the East wherein I have sat in complete quiet and peace although there might have been thousands of other people in that same structure. After what I might call "the cook's tour", I was shown to a central shaft that was guarded both by stationed clerks and by electrical means. We entered into a room that turned out to be the anti-room to another elevator. In this room we had to remove the clothing and put on a one-piece uniform that looked very strong and unplyable until it was touched; at once it then became quite flexible almost like silk. The next stage was to stand for a minute in a narrow passage at three different places where a neutralization, a polarization, and hermetic sterilization took place. When this was completed we entered into the <u>private chambers of Zemkla.</u>

The feeling was one of solemness and awe, yet there was a sence of light-hearted warmth. Much as a person feels prior to laughing due to natural cause. We went past and through several areas directly to what I guessed was the very top of the structure, and there found a single room which had a very long stately desk at one side. At this point I expected to find many seats on the far side but as Zemkla sat down it became clear that it was of the same uni-rail type as in the craft. Then after I had been invited to walk around behind the desk and behind Zemkla's chair the most amazing thing took place.

What I thought was a single large desk, was in reality the single set of remote controls for the entire pyramid. Apparently some button had been pushed and the table turned over exposing the electrical control console of the pyramid Zemkla had built. For several long minutes I found myself looking much the same I would guess, as the first person to see an automobile or an airplane fly, or a rocket ascent into the sky.

The tour was a thrilling experience, however so many new concepts in such a short span of time was difficult to grasp. It seemed as if Zemkla read my thoughts

*Plobeum--From the teachings of TABOF.

because he abruptly changed the subject by asking if I would like to have a meal. I was eager for the experience and said "yes". Afterwards I wondered what have I let myself in for? Zemkla took a program card about the size of a playing card from a file and inserted it into a slot. A light on the console lit up and after a short while the card came out and was replaced in the file. The reaction was a table and two benches raised from the floor on the west side of the room. Zemkla motioned to me and we walked over and sat down. At about the same time some very beautiful attendants came in from the only door on the north side, opposite the desk. Each brought on a crystal tray, a plate, and a tall thin glass. Both the plate and the service were of an opaque color and while the material was unknown, I was told that it was not metal or magnetic.

On the oval plate were four groups of food. It appeared to be one fourth pound of meat, three tablespoons of cooked vegetables, crisp salad and mushrooms. The drink had a bubbly feeling like ginger when swallowed. My host pointed to the mushrooms and told me in a very joking manner, "these are of a carbon base". The reason for this little joke was my search for plants that contained the Indole Ring producing elements, but not of a phosphorus base. He had been the one who guided the research which had been conducted on the various foods that were supposed to contain "some magical power". At that time he merely stated, "the working agent in the carbon based mushrooms is known to your planet as the Indole Ring". As I ate the meal I found I was analysing my own expanding awareness. It could have been mental suggestions of my own, but I felt that my sences perceived in a clearer manner. Before I realized it the meal was over and Zemkla invited me to see further evidence of the work he had done under the direction of Fahsz. As we left the highest and most stately chamber of the entire pyramid, I took a last look at the magnificent Golden Seal of Fahsz that hung over Zemkla's desk. I asked Zemkla if this was the highest room in the structure, he said "no". "There was the Apex room of Shel"; however he said nothing about it. Instead he described how all these developments had come about in the last three years.

Then he told me a little about his life before he had been contacted by Master Fahsz. It seems that he had been a politician and his job was to improve the conditions on their planet Selo. Because there was only one government on their planet their social and scientific progress worked together with co-operation. He told of his contact with Master Fahsz and of the origional assignment to align their planet Selo with the other four planets that had already completed the mission on their planets. These planets, one other, Prismov, his planet Selo, and Earth total seven planets. These are referred to as "The Planetary Seven".

Because the degree of scientific organization on their planet, coupled with centuries of living in harmony with each other, it was possible for Zemkla to do a great deal directly. The method that had been used was to contact each person on their planet by causing a newspaper which was printed by a machine in the home of each person to carry the story. By this means it was possible for a man in his position to give the full account in printed form and have it in every home on their planet the same day. He then followed it up with progress reports as he came to learn the full purpose of being contacted by "The Master Fahsz".

Although planet Selo has a twelve month year, the relative size of their planet is very much larger than their social needs. For this reason Zemkla asked for all persons intrested in this cultural movement to align their planet with the cosmos to move to a virgin continent. The job was to set up an entire city; self contained, self sufficient, to maintain all of the normal functions, adopt new techniques, and devices from the more advanced planets. The advanced "know-how" coming from four other planets, each of which is radically advanced from the others within the "Planetary Seven" helped to quickly bring about accomplishment. As this work proceeded many hundreds of thousands joined into the cultural improvement. By November of 1964 (Earth time), they had completed one Pyramid of Fahsz and their numbers were some 40,000 followers. Within the next few months that number doubled, tripled and finally, as a united people, the planet overcame "the forces of Alzur".

I was very eager to learn what changes that this had brought about and was very surprised at his answer. Firstly, it was a cultural advancement; social, scientific, religious together as part of a larger organization of other planets, solar systems and galaxies. As a new member they gained a great deal of information and this required major adjustments to the first generations. As they adapted new systems it was possible for extended communication and commerce with systems they didn't even dream existed. Not only was there communication with the other five planets of our planetary seven, but with six other groups of planets. For many ages these other planets and their civilizations have prepared for the additional planets to be added to the total of fourty-nine planets. This entire group of seven groups of seven planets each comprises a sector of space and are under the direct jurisdiction of Master Fahsz.

Just as the missionaries and explorers go into virgin areas, where pockets of men and women have lived for centuries, not knowing of anything beyond their tribes, so do these people in the spacecraft work. They know when the new planet is to be joined into the common work and then step in when and where they can do good, and prepare the people. By the time our planet is ready to accept the concept that we are not alone, the entire planet will have been surveyed by teams of workers coming to this planet in spacecraft. These craft have been seen by many more people than our government would like us to believe and y are willing to help us the way other groups helped them.

It is necessary that they select people from this planet and contact them to create a percentage of persons on the planet with an understanding. As eventual planetary commerce and cultural exchange will take place and this will speed it along, once it is out in the open. There is no real need of concealment of their activities from the average man and woman on the street; but they are not eager to place themselves in front of the weapons of our government when these weapons are being held by unstable, frightened, misinformed people that believe in "shoot first before asking questions".

They feel very sorry about the attitude and policies of our government in keeping the people enslaved to false information. Their main concern is in getting the job done as these things WILL COME ABOUT. Zemkla told me of some of the reactions that people had when their craft would come over head and appear to the people. He said that some would kneel down and worship them, others would think they were the devil, but the majority seemed to just run. For this reason they appeared very high in the sky where people could see them without having any personal feelings of fear. At the same time with the policy to "shoot it down" their people aboard the spacecraft refuse, except when ordered to come into full view.

Zemkla told me so many things, yet was wise enough to realize that all of this at once caused major changes in my thinking. He told me that over the years they had picked people from every social group, every country, and every walk of life. My reactions were only normal to be confronted with so much in so brief a period of time. I was told that in the future I would return many times to Selo before the pyramids of Fahsz were restored on the Earth.

On the return trip I was so caught up in my thoughts about what Zemkla had said that we were already outside the pyramid before I realized it. The crew was in the saucer: we entered and returned to the same spot in the hills where I had been instructed to drive. Apparently Zemkla knew that I was caught up in my thoughts about their planet and the vastness of their system. When we had landed I was again given the same arm-grip by Zemkla and we parted. The sleek craft shot straight upwards and in an instant its bright light appeared only as a fading star. Again I was left standing with my thoughts and the bulky recorder.

As I stood there I realized that regardless of how much evidence, be it recordings or photographs, it was impossible for many of the peoples of Earth to grasp the true significance of interplanetary contact. Governmental agencies seem to be organized only to hide, distort and restrict the knowledge from the people of this country. For these reasons it would only be a waste of time to report my experiences to the proper authorities. In all likelyhood it would only be dumped into the growing grave-yard of documentary UFO evidence. The important thing was to apply the knowledge that was given and try to show an example of the results of being in contact with an advanced civilization. For now at least I can see no reason to relate the story to those not interested. The local and national agencies of UFO "poo pooers." would only get another report to disregard and tax payers money would be spent declairing the sighting was wild geese, baseballs, or street lamps traveling at supersonic speeds. No, I would say nothing about it, although each contact has been carefully logged with all the data that is given.

VIMANAS from ATLANTIS

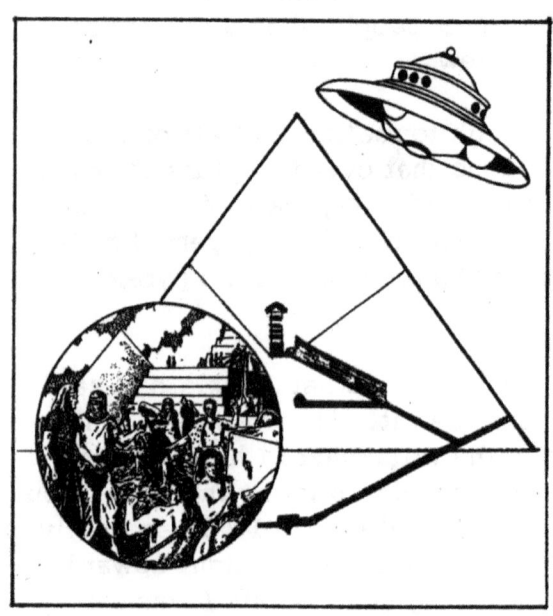

Let us start with the group which left Atlantis 50,000 years ago, however, bear in mind that history is only relative to a selected point in time; ultimately having no begining or ending as such.

In the last days of Atlantis there were those who had access to large spacecraft that could hold the entire population of a single planet. There is still some referances within libraries which have not been burned that refer to these devices as the "Cities of Shan". Those of Atlantis who knew of the destruction of both continents Atlantis and Lemuria, prepared for three groups. The first of these was instrumented into a large space device that left the planet as soon as it was ready. it was to orbit until the natural destruction came to an end. The second was under the charge of Master Nui: it was to remain here on the planet for the "New Age" wherein, the people of planet Earth would need every record, book, and device in the "Atlantian Time Capsule". The third group were those who were not of the scientific nature who left the planet, nor of the second who carried out the orders of TABOF under Master Nui. Many groups of people lived through the sinking of both major land areas and are divided as the "Tribes of Israel" today. It should be realized that in American Indian lore it is thought of as indian tribes, the Pacific Islanders think of everyone coming from the islands, etc.: in truth man orgionally migrated to the planet.

Of those who left our planet Earth, and have gone through many generations and do not resemble the orgional humans that started the trip. These space wanderers, who after 70,000 years, have forgotten their orgional purpose of their trip. They hopelessly seek a race of humans which exist in their appearance; searching the Universe in the living tomb of their own making. Nature has a rather exacting set of rules, and when man turns his back on the One Father he must return by his own effort.

In sharp contrast there were exceptions to this escape concept and many followed the directions of God's word through TABOF: these lived to write about the deluge.

* "Atlantis-God's Land", published by Galaxy **Press.**

Accounts speak of total destruction of Atlantis and her scientific temples of learning; however, there were many pockets of people who did not panic and under guidance lived through the holocaust. Bear in mind that the destruction was under the guiding hand of the One Father, having both direction and purpose. When the One Father released His wrath it was on the heads of those who had perverted light, life and love. Just as a farmer must return a crop into the soil, so did the Father; but only the guilty perished. Virgin lands were not disturbed and descendents of those people living God's law walk the planet today. The guiltless animals, birds, fish, and men were not punished for the selfish perversions of the few.

ATLANTIS AT ITS HEIGHT

" The Atlantis was the One Father's Kingdom on Earth and memories of it are in but a few minds. It flourished 150,000 years before the third coming of Anahsz. The people were taught to worship the One and Only Father in the true and correct manner, but they began to wander turning the powers given by the One Father to their own selfish gain, using the logos for the work of evil.

The priests of the Church of The Universe were given the power to plan future lives, and choose those with whom they would be associated in future lives. The high priests were given the powers of direct communication with the One Father. It came to pass that the people of The Atlantis attained a super knowledge which they used merely for their own personal gain, denying the One Father His due share. Master Fahsz appeared to the people and said, "All shall be given the means to enter the Kingdom who believes me and accept the coming of Anahsz as taught by the priests of the Church of The Universe.

Many wonderful things were told the peoples of that great civilization of Atlantis; however, it came to pass that the multitudes laughed at Master Fahsz and he left saying, "I am but a shadow in light." As the vibrational rate of those on the Atlantis and Lemuria was lowered by the One Father, great lightening and massacre resulted, which displeased the One Father. The One Father loosened His wrath and destroyed the Atlantis and Lemuria, taking with him the 144,000 where they would wait outside the "Gates to the Kingdom" for many ages."

* Atlantis: directly taken from the "Books of Fahsz".

THE LEMURA, LAST TO SINK

After the first group of people left the planet in an attempt to excape the wrath of the One Father, Atlantis sunk beneath the waters. Nui* (Noah) was placed in charge of saving all of the records and advances of civilization by putting them into an astounding device. This device was large enough not only to contain the combined accomplishments of Atlantis and Lemura; but all of the collective remnants of every major and minor civilization, including the history or the origional migration to this planet. It contains, in other words, all of the "seeds" needed for this planet to regain its former status, and enter into the Golden Age, or "New Age". When it came to pass that the Lemura must sink also, Nui boarded the device and remained therein. He, his co-workers, and every specie of life form went into the device. At a later date the animals were let out on certain land areas; Nui and his followers stepped out on the continent of Asia.

At the time of this landing on the China Coast, this Earth, speaking from a practical point of view, was "without life", "The Books of Fahsz".** Nui, whose name later became perverted into Noah led the people into starting a new life and history reports that it appears as if man sprung up from a single geographical area in Asia. The great pyramid of Peking, long since forgotten; but for a few minds is the only major land mark. The mystery of green stone and the monuments thereof have crumbled, just as the dedicated pyramid to the One Father in Peking, China has been torn down for its material.

NUI

The new civilization under the directorship of Nui re-formed on the coast of China, and was very different from Atlantis. The souls of mankind withheld from human form at that time are now returning to this Earth. The sacred symbol of the bee is marked upon those from Lemura. As each soul is released from their karmic lessons resulting from their rejection of the planetary Avatar of their age. On Asia science was maintained as a religious teaching with an attempt to hold togethe the basic principle for this, the "New Age". This was passed along by temple priests, yet the sacred science of Atlantis became less than "lip service" to the masses. The Great Seperation of the Flood has been the central theme written into books now all over the world showing that the "tribes" were spread throughout the world. Spread not due to being seperated as the land sank, but migrating to populate the world and taking with them some of the origional teachings. At one time

*"Voyage of Noah"--Galaxy Press.

**"The Books of Fahsz","here and there were extraordinary survivors, plant, animal, and human".

on this planet the Law of God and the known science was the same sacred covenant. Man bound himself to God by learning God's Law and living it. Now, centuries later, mankind sees no relationship between God the parent of this triune creation of joy, love, and light. All that remains are the few concepts about light, and this is understood as a cold unyielding mathematical quanity. The vast knowledge of Atlantis and Lemura remain in tact, awaiting the day when Anahsz will come again to receive this treasure now entrusted to the "high priests of Tibet".

While the main body of workers under the directions of Nui re-established themselves upon disembarking on the coast of China, many tribes of man, animal, and much of Africa remained above the water level and surprisingly survived. As the story of Nui, Atlantis, Lemura and the time capsule (ark) were told and retold, Nui became known as Noah. Today the evacuation of Lemura as planned by TABOF and directed by Nui has become the "Noah's Ark Story". The transporting of animals from one part of the world to another has been greatly expanded and the achievement of the One Father on Atlantis and Lemura through science and the books thereof removed from the story. This destruction and perversion of truth is done by those who serve Alzur, not as accidental mistakes, but as the continuing work of Alzdom.

Bear in mind that while some serve the One Father, God, there are others who serve the "prince of darkness", the devil, satan, or lucifer, believing that it is a better way of life. Still another group exists; those who sit idle glued to their chairs, mumbling, chanting, and procrastinating. These vidiots cycle between sleeping, eating, and sitting in the vain hope that someone else will do all of the spiritual work. However, the workers are paid, not the sleepers. These "manna boys" prefer the bedtime stories those of Alzdom tell of the perverted truth. By constantly druging their senses with indole poisons they unwittingly remain spiritually asleep.

By accentuating the "eight indole poisons" the forces of Alzur keep the population of this planet in a state of stupor. There is no real need for work on their part at this point; however, as they have control of the Alzbrums within a percentage of the population of the planet, it would be fairly easy to bring about the crucifixion, emtombment, or death of anyone who might accomplish too much.

For this reason many workers have incarnated on this planet at this time. Member planets of TABOF in this sector stand by giving ample evidence of their exisance to cameras, radar, and other measuring tools of science which are managed by experts who have a difficult time in discovering anything beyond the range of their own noses.

The facts that science cannot reconcile into their data are: The history of this planet, back to the "Flood", and the "Day the Earth Stood Still". Present history of our sector of space which does not have any gaps of lost records. TABOF, which from a purely physical point of view contains the greater population of this sector of space, who are interested in <u>helping</u> those workers who will work in their own behalf by interplanetary culture exchange.

THE COSMIC BEING

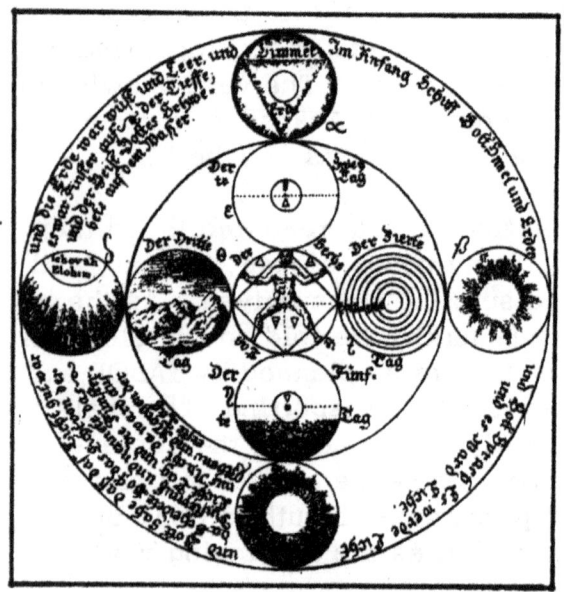

Man was created, or more exactly, was reflected by the One Father through the principles of Light. The body of the Father on the physical plane of existence is light; however, light should not be the object of worship. In the begining, which was never, light was made manifest from the center of the universe. Strictly speaking the core projects constantly and is the expanding universe. There are three major aspects to its pulsating ray: (1) Eiyadas, (2) Ejira, and (3) Hemlo. These strike our Earth with a beam of cosmic light one mile in width between each of six vortexes, and are enlarged around the vortex center. As this beam radiates to every part of the universe and passes through the 76 planes of existence before striking our world, it projects into manifestation everything that is within the core. It is as if there were mirrors set in a barber shop so that the reflection can be seen to trail off, getting smaller and smaller. It is very like this that the cosmic being is manifested into existence. On each plane, planet, or screen that which is projected follows the three principles of light, i.e., absorbtion, transmission, and reflection.

We on this planet provide a life cycle system based upon the carbon principle; therefore, all that is projected to our planet manifests according to the carbon base principle. The planet beneath our feet is expanding as is the entire universe and the points corresponding to the human chuckra are the six vortex points. The seventh is the planet itself. The human being as manifested on this planet is built on the carbon cycle: the six races of man are but offshoots of the one race of man, the human race. The seventh race is the universal race. Zemkla is from another planet also based upon the carbon cycle and is of the universal race. Characteristics are seen in pre-Egyptian art and throughout Indian lore of the seventh or "root race of man".

The twelve tribes are but the six aspects, both male and female of the cosmic being, which cannot be affected regardless how many times man divides himself. At the end of each age, which is never, those members of the universal race are free to return to the Kingdom of God whence they came.

The key to the entire matter, from a scientific or structural level, is the indole. Some years ago the author was given radically new data on the indole which he studied in lab tests. This methodology was published in a book called, "Gateway to Superconsciousness-The Drug Experience Without Drugs". He was pounced upon from every quarter due to the total lack of public information. In order to comply with conditions at the time it was suggested that the word drug be removed from the book due to the "LSD witchhunt". The key point to the entire subject is the indole, although the scientific world has not as yet come to that realization.

Indoles, under certain (normal) conditions are produced by the body and are the working agent which causes "psychic function". It is a shame that the study of this aspect of man's body has been so abused that our government has created laws restricting "LSD". The prime issue is the INDOLE, not LSD. To make a blanket statement as to how every human body can be transformed back to the origional structure would require a life-time work; but the catalyst is fairly easy to understand.

Foods can be broken down into two groups: Life producers and death producers. The human system is built such that many poisons can be introduced into the body without a quick sickness or death. It has been conditioned to endure many forms of poison and this in turn reduces the percentage of indoles within any given body. Those in the "New Age" think of the sixth and seventh senses as way out mysterious powers akin to the dark ages, the alchemist, and witchcraft. Just as a flashlight would probably have brought about a quick death at the stake at that time, a healthy body at this time is subject to social austeration. While Di Venchi had to draw the idea of the helicopter through the use of a mirror, to avoid discovery; today vehicles passing through our smoggy atmosphere are written off as "swamp gas".

The main issue is that we are part of the universal race of man, a reflection of the cosmic being and there are specific universal truths which we could apply. As the New Age is upon us, we must choose life or death, peace or war, fact or swamp gas. As a man thinkes, so is he.

In respect to Zemkla, the author is attempting to introduce a cultural exchange between planets; however, the first issue comes under the heading, "Health and Sanitation".

The arguments presented which oppose these concepts come from the local witch doctors who with-held the discovery of Dr. A. Baeyer; who in 1866 discovered and named the INDOLE. It would seem unwise to allow information to reach the general public that may remove disease from a system of economics based on war.

To make issue as to the type and style of shoe strings Zemkla may wear does not seem to be the main point of interplanetary cultural exchange. Zemkla has most graciously accepted our customs and has startled this author by appearing at public lectures wearing a business suit; however to avoid detection he does not, nor do any of TABOF wear clothes that would cause people to think they were not of this world.

If interested, all a person needs to do is take notice of which popular foods are poisons to the human body and not eat them. This one step will do more than any other single act. Some of these, our "Food and Drug Laws," have labeled as "Hazardous to your Health".

There is no point of repeating material which can be found in "Gateway" as the method of redeveloping revitalizing, and spiritualizing the body may be found therein.

The cosmic being is projected as an image and likeness to this planet; however, each being has free will and choice as to what materials that manifestation will contain. They can be of the universe or of the anti-universe, of matter or anti-matter, or of God or anti-God.

The vimanas, flying saucers, or spacecraft come to our planet not as entertainment for an otherwise bored civilization, but to bring a contact with advanced science and cultural development which could enhance the life of every manifest cosmic being on this Earth.

SOUL-MATES AND TWIN-RAYS

Those who are now living on this planet are of one of two major groups: teachers or students. Althought there are many degrees or levels within these groups the largest percent are doing nothing for various reason. This does not take into account those born on other planets and brought here by vehicles to work among us, for they could pass for a normal earth human, except for one factor...they are healthy.

Zemkla represents planet Selo, yet there are 17 other men and women from his planet stationed on our Earth. Just as we send our people into another nation as "The Peace Corp", fourty-eight other planets send TABOF to this interplanetary colony to avert disaster.

Another group of workers are those "New Agers" who have passed the tests of stability and have had physical contact with those from other planets. In most cases people refuse to speak of their UFO experience because they fear the result. This is no small issue for what would you do if you (alone) saw a UFO, spoke to a member of their crew, or physically entered for a short hop...no doubt you would never speak of it. Unfortunately our government has ordered the de-bunking of all UFO data therefore, do not be surprised if they are unhappy when you break their bubble.

Soul-mates and twin-rays find themselves traveling from planet to planet within the seven groups helping each other over the difficulties of planet life. Some travel as Zemkla in a physical flying saucer just as we travel from country to country via aircraft. After having overcome the trials on their planet some wish to bring the Gospel of the returning Christ (Anahsz) to planet Earth.

The appearance of the UFO's in our skies was the start of a more active attempt to assist us in accomplishing the mission before we brought about an all-out atomic holocaust; destroying human life from this planet. It is impossible to effect a cultural exchange to have just one person recieve material from Selo or another enlightened source. This cultural exchange will have to be from "people to people". Many more contacts will have to be made than is realized. Some of our people are so neurotically out of balance that just a fleeting light buzzing overhead is enough to send them to the "happy farm". Others, like Albert Einstein can endure not only contact, but pass along a small amount of data. None the worse for it either...so long as nothing is said as to where said data came from. Most of us however, fall in the middle range. We can endure such an experience, but even so, dare not to speak of it.

This was the plight of this author as well, for as he delved into the "Secrets of Life", asking the same questions that men and women have asked for centuries, he found answers that could not be refuted. The quest could be divided into two phases: seeking the truth, and trying to live with the truth once found. The Yoga teachers speak of this planet as Evedia Maya-World of Illusion. Rightly so, for to find reality is considered folly to the patron of incarnate entrapment.

Most people function on the emotional level, those seeking the truth, enlightenment are functioning in the mind. When functioning purely in the physical, there are no other requirements than those of staying alive, such as occurs even in sleep.

If you raise your indole count high enough to come out from this self-induced sleep do not expect to find the fellow sleeper of Earth happy to be awakened from his dreams. You can break your own bubble and find reality, but the slightest attempt to awaken your sleeping friends, neighbors, and relatives will meet sharp disapproval when your efforts pass the point of entertainment.

Realizing this the author elected to try to disprove his findings only to discover that as he maintained a high indole count another world came into view. Soon daily communication with TABOF was possible and a wealth of knowledge came to him to be put out into book form. Then a school teacher, it would not have been wise to "speak out" so data piled up. Soon he studied of the attempts of others contacted by TABOF, and eventually went into monastic life in the East to have the complete teachings given. This account is treated completely in another book, "Contact With The Masters"*, which goes into detail on how he was graduated from the schools of the East as Chela, to a Mahatma Rishi Guru, to become the student and friend of Zemkla.

TRIAL by POLYGRAGH

The author after his contact in 1957, elected "not to speak of his contacts". Following instructions he wrote and lectured in the New Age-Metaphysical field without openly speaking of these "saucer contacts". After many years of silence Zemkla

* "Contact With The Master"-published by Galaxy Press.

finally released him to speak about them on October 26, 1965: however he chose not to do so. Shortly afterwards while speaking to the "New Age Questors", sponsored by Florance Verrico on Oriental Pholosophies the "cat got out of the bag" when the question period began.

Directly word got around and Hal Wilcox was asked if he would appear on the Joe Pyne Show, and also take a lie detector test. Upon making a contact with Zemkla, Hal was reminded that on Selo many people made known their willingness to take part in the interplanetary culture exchange as given them by the Council Interplanetay Seven and TABOF. It was therefore suggested that the same pattern be applied here on this planet. With the hopes of finding other people who could handle the UFO question, Hal agreed to the TV appearance and the polygraph test.

The Central Bureau of Investigation was on hand to give the test commonly called the "Lie Detector Test". This is a method through which perceptible physical reactions are recorded on a long scroll or paper. Electrodes on the hands measure sweating as an increased flow of electric current. A rubber tube around the chest measures respiration changes. An inflated tube around the upper arm denotes blood pressure and pulse changes. These variations are drawn on a moving graph by a set of ink pens. Thus polygraph in Greek means "many writings".

The lie detector relates such accurate information that the use of it raises a basic constitutional question as the Fifth Amendment says, "no one may be compelled to bear witness against himself". But by the same token it can prove the truthfulness of a given statement made by a person taking such a test.

The only condition Zemkla gave was to be very careful about how the evidence was to be presented. It should be given to the people over the TV, and not twisted into pure entertainment. While a free pamphlet has been prepared containing the full transcription of the show called "Trial by Polygraph", a brief description is as follows.

The show started in typical fashion: Hal Wilcox was the first guest of the evening, and was introduced as a minister of the Church of The Universe. After a short discussion Hal and the Central Bureau of Investigation were dismissed from the camera's eye. At the end of the show Hal was brought back and the trap was sprung. Joe Pyne made an issue as to what company manufactured the uniform worn by Zemkla and then went on to examine in great detail the shoes he wore. Of principle issue were the shoe strings and their exact color.

Joe tried to find Hal's weak point however, was confronted with three statements backed by a polygraph test. The audience roared when Hal was again brought back to be seen by a good percentage of the American public. The questions that were thrown at Hal were, "was there a hot-dog stand on planet Selo?"; "What did superman say to you?", and "I am Zemkla, what do you think about that?" The crowd howled and Hal laughed along with them--not offering any information other than the statements which were backed by the polygraph test and that a vast amount of information had been given to pass along to the people of Earth that were serious. This number may very well become larger as time passes because Congress has set aside funds for the investigation of the UFO question. The "swamp gas bit" was thrown around on the show and it ended by a last attempt at debunking the entire affair by presenting the polygraph test result. It was shown to the American public in true Pyne fashion--upside down and backwards. The report of the qualified operator although slippery and vague was POSSITIVE. Yes, Hal was telling the truth, he did see Zemkla, enter his craft, and visit a planet named Selo. The show ended, or more exactly stated, the power was turned off and Hal remained some hours talking to the interested crowd...without Pyne.

Creed of Fahsz

"I am Fahsz. I am the servant of the Father and Brsgv and the master of Anahsz who permeates the universe on the physical plane of Existence. On my right hand there are seven stars and on my left hand seven golden pyramids. The seven pyramids are the seven steps to Fahsz through Anahsz, and the seven stars the seven inner teachers. Write of all the things I have told you and the things you have seen in the Kingdom or marvelled at during the shel. There are two great forces in the universe of which only my deserving acceptors can be aware. These are: Hal and Shel: the force of light and the creative force. You are to create a temple of many pyramids which shall be opened unto all who receive Anahsz.and the one who is at the right hand of Anahsz. These two have received shel: no others have. Follow my teachings and you shall live, obey my acceptors and you shall permeate the universe. The one who sits at the right hand of Anahsz is his opposite number; each of these has an opposite number who reflects as a mirror. On the earthly plane these two are called Anahsz and Zekhariah."

PROJECT EARTH

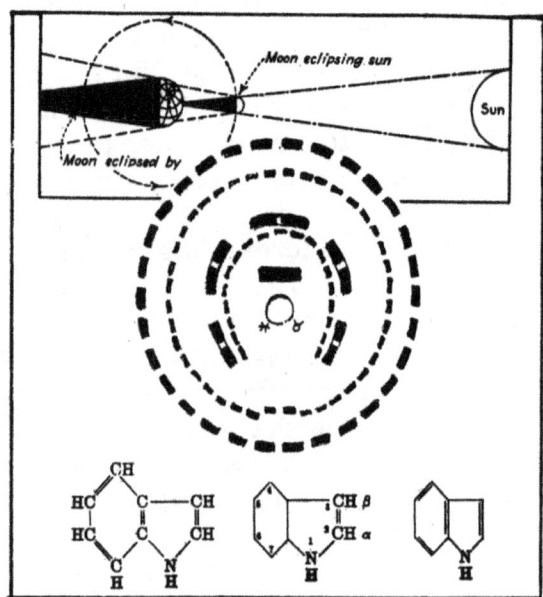

On the great planetary conjunction of February 5, 1962, the "New Age" started for the last three planets of Group VII. This means that a cycle of work has started, for as "time turns" we will either finish the job in the allotted time, or all go down together. Matter is either in place or out of place according to the vibration level of each being. The graduation class of Earth will move into the next frequency and leave behind those who are not ready to continue through reincarnation until they too are spiritually developed.

Now the books of Revelations have been opened and the veil removed. The Alzur force will burn itself off this Earth as two thirds destroy each other.

Satan, the black angel is very active on this Earth at this time. Those who serve the prince of hell crave destruction, just as the children of the One Father serve Him by acts of free will and love. Certain signs have been given us to look for in the sky when the reflection of God will be made manifest and seen by every man that has hope of salvation in him. Those who are prepared will know that which is about to come to pass, the majority will panic. Many have been tricked into serving Alzdom on this planet and will reject their own salvation as they cling to perverted teachings.

When the appearance and the release will occur is not known, but it will be at the END of the struggle. The holocaust is now at hand and now is the time to choose who you will serve. Right now within your body are indoles, these can hold Alzbrums from functioning; however to do so, one Olbrum is required to contain two Alzbrums. (See Indole Chart) The Olbrums are the small percent of your spiritual being that may under certain conditions enter your body. The re-entry of your spiritual being into your soul and body is the second birth of spirit. This superconsciousness will come into your being when the method* is followed and no indole poisons are put in your body. Indole production will be on the increase. As they increase, eventually enough will enter your physical body to balance the Alzur force of your body. At this point your own God-created spiritual being can control its earthly counterpart the body.

To lose control of your being one only needs to take any one of the first seven indole poisons into their body as these destroy indoles in proportion to the poison

---

* The method - from "Gateway to Superconsciousness".

ingested. **The eighth poison: PIG, PORK, BACON, HAM, SAUSAGE, PORK BOLOGNA, PORK WEINERS, PIG FEET, PIG TAIL, PIG HEAD, BOAR, SOW, HOG,** any part, top bottom, front, back--cooked, burnt, raw, is PIG and will destroy totally your indoles.

The human body is a wonderful electro-biological organism and can adjust to many extremes. We have found that we can inoculate it so that it will ward off disease or fight it effectively. This principle has been used very effectively with respect to the indole poisons for at a very early age most people are given small dosages of indole poisons so that as they grow older they can tolerate large dosages. It will work just as a booster shot later in life for so long as a person takes small dosages of indole poisons he will maintain his insulation against this poison. The only problem is that he unwittingly insulates himself from allowing his sixth and seventh senses to develop.

There are two approaches to this issue: scientific and metaphysical. The first would say that under certain conditions when indolic substance increases in the body and that extra-sensory perceptions are manifested. Metaphysicians who do not demand to know the exact sub-atomic action of the indole structure in their body and are quite happy to simply learn the causal factor which allows for their controlled ESP functions. This subject is delved into at great length in the book "LSD Foods"*. However, our point here is you are now choosing your physical, mental, and spiritual limitations by introducing death producing elements into your being--knowingly or unknowingly.

Each person is deciding their own fate by allowing the overbalance of alzbrums in their body and the destruction of indoles. The spiritual being is linked to the physical body by these indoles and the percentage of the spiritual being in the body depends on the number of indoles. Imagine, if you will, a puppet and two puppeteers. One puppeteer we will call good and the other evil. The good one has a string which connects to every indole that has been charged; while the evil puppeteer has a string to each alzbrum. Both attempt to control the body the good one through "free will and choice", and the evil one through force. Thinking of the entire physical human body as it is on this planet, only about one pint of it, the indolic substance, flowing along with the blood contains the GOD self. So the Prince of Darkness needs only to sit back and watch to win.

People living in upstream areas of the six planetary vortexes will have a strengthening of God force containing the "free will and choice". Those down stream will find a rather sudden outbreak of crime, and personal stress when the vortexes are activated. It is not without reason that so many of the world's churches have sprung up within the upstream areas and various forms of crime in the back wash area. Further the point where the two forces meet, half of the land area between two different vortex points, planetary wars have been fought. People tending to do

*"LSD Foods"--A book explaining the causes for the "Drug Experience" and how it can be induced through eating certain foods.

As the One Father restores the majesty of Anahsz on this planet so all will see, it is important that we protect our bodies with the light barrier of the indoles. We are told of these times from the Books of Fahsz as follows: "Man the ramparts, watch the road, gird your loins and collect all your strength". The One Father intends that all see the red shield of the Father's mightly man. "His words are clothed in scarlet, the chariots flash like flame and are mustered in array". Spacecraft darting in to pick up those New Agers who are the children of the One Father. "The chargers rush to and fro through the square, they gleam like torches" (the Air Force swamp gas). "They dart like lightening, the members of the Church of The Universe are summoned. They stumble as they go, they hasten to the wall" (pathway of the vortexes) "the mantlet is set up, the river gates are opened, the palace is in dismay".

This spectacular description of the "planetary graduation" is given from Volume IX of the seventy-six books of Fahsz.

Now is the time to build into your bodies the required indoles which is allowing "Mother nature" control simply by not eating indoles poisons. So you have conscious control to bring your own devine spirit, give up your soul and reason and serve serve alzdom.

THE INSTITUTE OF PARAPSYCHOLOGY

There was time when the author was not allowed to speak about where he got his information, however his psychic abilities and work as a spiritual healer brought many private students to his door. Permission was granted that he teach the same methods used on more advanced planets provided he did not tell where their concepts came from. As a school teacher working towards degrees in educational administration, he planned a curriculum such that any adult student enrolling would be certain of certain specific ability after a pre-determined semester hours of work. These classes were taught in a very successful manner speaking of accomplishment; however one teacher can reach only so many students and such an approach is impractical.

This data as taught in the Institute of Parapsychology, founded by the present director, Hal Wilcox, are to be given to all seeking truth, and willing to do something. All too often we think that hearing an idea is the same as applying that idea into daily life--this is not so. Thought, word, and deed, work together to bring about fruition into this world of material form.

The first statement that was made in these classes was,"The first step is to gain control of your biological functions. Before anything can be started two things have to happen: (1) cleaning the body, and (2) proper diet." It is important that you prepare the body such that the spiritual being can enter into the clay and be re-born as the Master said,"of the spirit". This re-birth process, taught in private classes, was given by the Church of the Universe and has been published in the book called "Going Up!". This name, for the method of consciously entering the spiritual being into the physical body and travelling in spirit form, was named "Going Up!" by the origional deciples in Tenri City, Japan.

The complete works of the Books of Fahsz will be available through Galaxy Press and as material is translated will be offered for your future spiritual development. While these methods open the pineal gland and allow the LSD experience, these methods are not intended for the profane and the courious. It was only after much pleading did the agent of TABOF, Zemkla, release the method as given in the book "Gateway". Now after many have read and accepted the earlier teaching, further instruction will be given.

Zemkla's contact was intended to pass along the methods for spiritual attainment for all New Agers who seek Light and Truth. It is hoped that small groups will band together and apply this spiritual and scientific knowledge in practical life situations. Then as this number grows and the acceptance of the interplanetary cultural exchange. takes place, monographs for personal instruction will be available.

WHY SAUCERS ARE IN OUR SKIES

The first and lowest phase of the Saucer Story is for people of Earth to look up, see mysterious UFO's, and deduce that they are from other planets. While it may be true that now experimental craft are being built on the Earth this is only because the USSR captured a two-man device. The origional concept is still in tack ,i.e., a more intelligent race of man is flying about over head in a saucer-shaped craft. It was thought that by now the general public of the Earth would have realized this truth regardless what form of debunking each nation might use. It is a paradox that the leading nation, the United States of America, in scientific matters and space exploration would spend the public tax dollar in educating our people that these spacecraft are "spring thaws releasing trapped gases resulting from decomposing organic material in swamps and these have produced the objects seen from Australia to Michigan in a flurry of errie UFO sightings".

While it seems hard to believe that adults can allow themselves to believe that these gasses can achieve weightlessness, dematerialize, move from zero miles per hour to speeds of 5,000 miles per hour without any time lag for acceleration, follow aircraft and missles , and right angle turns at speeds of more than 5,000 miles per hour, some swamp gas!!

AIR FORCE REGULATION NO. 200-2	*AFR 200-2 1-2 Department of the Air Force Washington, 14 Sept. 1959
Intelligence UNIDENTIFIED FLYING OBJECTS (UFO)	
This regulation establishes the responsibility and procedure for reporting information and incidence on unidentified flying objects (UFO) and for releasing pertinent information to the general public.	

The author has given his life to finding the ancient records of Fahsz here on this planet and attempting to bring about the restoration of the Oracle of Delphi on this Earth. The staff is at present part-time helpers, who are trying to assist Zemkla and TABOF to bring advanced metaphysical wisdom to the New Agers on this planet.

In the research department modern alchemy formula for the Elixer of life, the philosopher's stone and transmutation principles are being delved into; however, there are no funds for these projects other than profits from these publications and donations to the Church of the Universe.

As the program expands so will the material entrusted be released to sincere seekers of truth. Truths of such vital nature are to be shared by all and not locked in vaults to rot.

Zemkla came from planet Selo on a mission to help those who would accept such help and bring with him the necessary tools with which we must work out our salvation. While Fahsz is the messenger to the One Father he is also the Sector Commander and has ordered Zemkla to offer this help. It will remain for us to decide for ourselves if we will restore our own being into a spiritual being, such as the Father created or be plowed under as fertilizer for the next civilization.

Ino Pazis Gnurum

Hal Wilcox Through Newspaper Articles
(1951-1993)

West Los Angeles Independent (West Los Angeles, California)

13 Sep 1951, Thu. Page 19

HAROLD (Hal) WILCOX, son of Mr. and Mrs. Harold M. Wilcox of 11726 Tennessee Ave., is home on leave from the US Army for two weeks before flying to Ft. Lawton, Seattle, for embarkation to Yokohama, Japan.

The soldier has lived in West Los Angeles for 13 years. He was graduated from University High School in the winter class of 1950. He was the only boy in his class with a perfect attendance record through junior and senior high schools.

While at Unihi Hal was a lieutenant in the ROTC, a member of the band and orchestra, and the gym team. He was ROTC band leader and won a scholarship at Brown's Military Academy at San Diego.

Hal enlisted in the Army last March. Most recently stationed at Ft. Mason, San Francisco, Hal was a member of the band with an MOS rating. He is being sent to Japan with others from Ft. Mason with high recommendations from the band warrant officer. He was offered a lieutenant's rank in the regular army but since his work has been in bands, he preferred to make that his Army work.

Hal is a member of Westwood Liberal Arts Chapter Order of DeMolay.

Convention At harmony Grove To Attract 800
Times-Advocate (Escondido, California)
01 Jul 1964, Wed. Page 1

Convention At Harmony Grove To Attract 800

Approximately 800 to 900 persons are expected to attend various sessions of the five-day convention of the Borderland Sciences and Research Associates at Harmony Grove this weekend, Mrs. Fred Rannenberg, financial secretary of the Harmony Grove Spiritualist Association, said Wednesday. Riley Crabb of Vista is director of the convention.

The convention will get underway Thursday evening with a gathering of what Mrs. Rannenberg termed the "early birds" to hear Fred Kimball of Los Angeles discuss "Demonstrations and Communications Between Man and Animals." Kimball's talk will start at 8:15 p.m. in the auditorium at Harmony Grove.

Principal speaker during the five-day meeting will be Joseph Busby of Sussex, England, who will give his first talk at 11 a.m. Sunday on "The Emerging Plan of the Forces of Light." Sunday evening, Busby will discuss "The Plan of the Universal Temple of the SUN." SUN stands for "Spiritual United Nations."

Friday's program will be highlighted by talks by Sepora Dobbins of Tucson, Ariz., who will speak on "Echo From the Future." She is an astrologist. Other speakers and their topics for that day are Clark Wilkeson, who recently returned from Hawaii, on "Aloha Land of the Kahunas" and Dr. Nelson Decker on "Healing Hands of the Blackfoot Indians." He is a chiropractor.

The hieroglyphics on the rocks in the Harmony Grove area will be interpreted Saturday by Lloyd Flowers who will speak on "Migration to the Americas in the First Century." A. E. Van Vogt, president of the California Association of Dianetics, will speak on "The Five-Pointed Star of Success."

On Saturday, Larry and Kathleen Chatterton will tell of the "Splendors of Greece and Pompeii." Chatterton is a Los Angeles radio station announcer. On Sunday, in addition to Busby's talk, Hal Wilcox, who spent three years in a monastery in Japan, will tell of his experiences.

The Harmony Grove association will open a six-week session on July 12, Mrs. Rennenberg said.

Club President Claims UFOs Spotted Over Reno

Nevada State Journal (Reno, Nevada)
11 Jul 1966, Mon. Page 3

SAUCERY — The Amalgamated Flying Saucer Clubs of America concluded a three-day convention in Reno last night and, in an effort to send them off happily, Journal photographer Lonnie Peck whipped up this bit of a spoof by double-exposing his film on an inside lamp fixture and an outdoor sign. Gabriel Green, president of the AFSCA and director of the convention, had earlier expressed his hope that a flying saucer would manifest itself to the general public in Reno during the convention. (Journal Photo)

By JACK STEVENSON
Journal Staff Reporter

A good deal of really "far out" talk was concluded last night in the Centennial Coliseum where nearly 1,000 true believers — and a number of non-believers — congregated for the Third National Convention of the Amalgamated Flying Saucer Clubs of America.

The three-day convention closed Sunday night on a note of mixed emotion on the part of its director, Gabriel Green, of Los Angeles.

Green, who is also the full-time president of the AFSCA, said that the convention was not as financially successful as had been hoped. But he hastened to add that the club's reception in the Reno area was "warm, friendly, and dignified."

He said that although greater attendance could have been hoped for, those who came treated us with sincerity and respect . . . and came to the meetings with open minds and an apparently sincere effort to understand what is going on in outer space.

Green, who says he has personally seen about 90 flying saucers, including two during his stay here in Reno, said that "we were hoping that they (flying saucers) might give us a little boost during our convention by manifesting themselves over Reno — but we had no such luck."

The head saucerer said that "a select group amongst us did receive a prophecy that saucers would appear . . . and on the night of my arrival I sighted a dark, circular, slow moving object in the sky. About 30 minutes later, a group of us sighted a similar object over the Reno Airport and it flew slowly over with a jerky sort of motion — bobbing up and down.

"There is little use in my reporting these things," Green said, "and many other believers are now also reticent to make such reports because they are simply subject to certain derision.

"What we need to gain momentum in this movement is reports of sightings from 'non-believers' who have never seen a flying saucer before. As it is, only about five million people in the United States have seen them," Green said.

One of the final speakers at the convention was a Hal Wilcox, of Los Angeles, who opened and closed his presentation with a mystic chant accompanied by a salaam-like gesture which put his fingertips to forehead and thumbs to upper lip.

A goodly number of people in the audience of about 200 persons joined him in the ritual incantation.

The cant itself was contained in a 36-page booklet which Wilcox offered for sale.

The booklet, titled "Gateway to Superconsciousness," embodies much of the knowledge which Rev. Wilcox claims to have gained in an Oriental monastary and on a subsequent trip through outer space to a planet called Celo.

Part of Rev. Wilcox's thesis

"I realize there are a number of non-believers," Wilcox said amiably Sunday night, "but if you're writing about any of this you might mention that I was recently on coast-to-coast television — and I took a polygraph (lie detector) examination right there and passed it with flying colors.

"Some experiences are difficult to believe without experiencing them yourself — but believe me," Wilcox concluded, "I've been there."

Wilcox said he received his ordination following studies in the Spiritual Development Foundation, and the Temple of Divine Wisdom, both in Los Angeles, and a monastic period of one and one-half years in a temple at Tenri City, Japan.

His first ride to outer space, he said, was in 1963 when he was picked up in a space vehicle near the Los Angeles Coliseum.

Rev. Wilcox said he was formerly a teacher in the Los Angeles school department but has, in recent years, dedicated himself to the teaching of parapsychology.

Jet Crashes In Yosemite

ALAMEDA, Calif. (UPI) — An unidentified Marine Air Reserve pilot, flying a Navy Skyhawk jet from Alameda Naval Air Station here, crashed Sun-

The head saucerer said that "a select group amongst us did receive a prophecy that saucers trip through outer space to a planet called Celo.

Part of Rev. Wilcox's thesis deals with the origin of hallucinogenic drugs which, according to his speech originated on planets other than earth. He said a visit from outer space was made some 500 years ago, and vegetables left behind by the extra-terrestial visitors were subsequently cultivated by American Indians.

On his visit to the planet Celo, Wilcox said, he was given a vegetable with the same hallucinogenic effects as the drug L.S.D. "but without its drawbacks." The booklet also deals with such drugs as peyote, mescalin, mushrooms, and "plants from other planets."

The booklet then goes on to describe "The Method" and way of life which Wilcox regularly teaches in his Los Angeles headquartered Institute of Parapsychology.

DEATHS

Death Notices

FERRIS — Friends are invited to attend services for Minnie Ferris on Tuesday at 3 p.m at the Home Chapel of Ross, Burke and Knobel Mortuary with Rev. Roy Weigon and Rebecca Lodge officiating. Private cremation to follow.

Neil McVicar

Funeral services for Neil W. McVicar will be conducted at 2 p.m. Tuesday in the Smith Valley Methodist Church.

Mr. McVicar, 79, died Saturday in a Yerington hospital.

Burial will be in the Hillcrest Cemetery, Smith Valley.

Citrus students in Hollywood
Band and drill team in parade

Daily News-Post (Monrovia, California)
15 Nov 1967, Wed. Page 2

The Citrus College band and drill team will appear in the Santa Claus Lane parade on Wednesday, Nov. 22, in Hollywood.

Selection for participation in the 36th annual official opening of the Southern California holiday season represents a high honor for the year-old Citrus College band. D. Joe Searcy of the college music department is director.

The 56-member band will march in new uniforms of blue and white, the college colors.

Cheryl Wilkinson of Azusa, holder of a number of drum major championships, heads the group. Andree Lacy of Duarte is majorette.

The college precision drill team, comprised of 25 coeds, is under the leadership of Virginia Grebing of Azusa.

Baumberger, Sheila King, Trill Rowley and Hal Wilcox.

Instrumentalists from Azusa are Richard Armenta, Kenneth Hartwell, Peter Roloff, Fred Salce, Jorge Alaniz, William Vasquez, Cheryl Wilkinson, Jerrie Powell, Katherine Smith, Dorothy Munday, Michael Adams, Sue Graham and Emily Fiehler.

Monrovia students are Arthur Gutierrez, Gary McClain, William Mohr, Michael Pecanic, Dave Prudden, Danny Mahnkin, Linda Nylander, Cheryl Williams, Marilyn Clark and Sally Pfeiffer.

Completing band membership

Monrovia gets $5,908 fees

are Steve Baroni, John Chidester, Linda Johnson, Andree Lacy and Keith Pashby, Duarte; Craig Bashore, Claremont; Larry Gelhar, Carl Sommer, Tom Shrouder, Richard Siddal and Marie Klein, El Monte; Linda Rawlins, Arcadia.

Drill team members are Teresa Tapia, Virginia Grebing, Jane Rathburn, Pam Gunning, Sandi Glasscock, Cathi Dodd, Leigh Lindquist, Carol Curtis and Nancy Roberts, Azusa; Nita Flegal, Marilyn Waters, Mary Schaeffer and Nancy Roberts, Glendora; Marilyn Clark, Deborah Myles, Sonja Bowen, Barbara Ward, Donna Lindsey, Donna Kimbrough, Karen Kaufmann and Barbara Klein, Monrovia; Kathy MacKenzie and Susan Moor, Arcadia; Carol Earl, Duarte, and Dawn Elson, Claremont.

Wearing new uniforms, Bob Evans of Glendora, (left) and Ken Hartwell of Azusa engage a light moment during a rehearsal for their appearance No. 22 in the Santa Claus Lane parade in Hollywood.

The trophy to be received for taking part in the Santa Claus Lane parade will join the band's growing collection, which includes a major award in the 1966 Junior Rose Bowl parade three months after the band was organized. On the same occasion, Miss Wilkinson was named champion drum major.

Recent off-campus band appearances have included a demonstration appearance in the Chaffey high school band tournament last month in Ontario, when Searcy headed a staff of 35 judges in the annual competition.

Members of the college band from Glendora are Dave MacDonald, Lanore Campbell, Robert Evans, Robert Figueroa, Richard Heagle, William Huff, Richard Isbell, Madeline Martin, Tom McCullough, Terry Paananen, Louise Rice, Craig Rochette, Carl Webb, Wayne Wilhite, Mark Rogers, Deborah Monson, Harold Baldwin, Susan

LECTURES

The Los Angeles Times (Los Angeles, California)

30 Jul 1972, Sun. Page 489

FRIDAY

"THE PSYCHOLOGY OF IMMORTALITY: A JUNGIAN VIEW OF CHINESE YOGA" by Dr. Stephan Hoeller, Southwest Counseling Service, 7323 S. Crenshaw Blvd., 8 p.m.

"MEDIUMS, CLAIRVOYANCE, PREDICTION AND TELEPATHY" by Hal Wilcox, Brookside Country Club, 5301 San Vicente Blvd., 8:15 p.m.

SATURDAY

The Los Angeles Times (Los Angeles, California)
01 Oct 1972, Sun. Page 536

FRIDAY

"CONGRESS AND THE AMERICAN PEOPLE" by Edward J. Avila, Memorial Branch Library, 4625 W. Olympic Blvd., 10 a.m.

"ISSUES AND QUESTIONS FOR THE 18-YEAR-OLD VOTER ON BALLOT PROPOSITIONS AND U.S. FOREIGN POLICY," discussion, Panorama City Branch Library, 14345 Roscoe Blvd., Panorama City, 7:30 p.m.

"EXPLORING THE INNER AND OUTER LIMITS OF SELF-AWARENESS" by Bill Sanford, First Unitarian Church, 2936 W. 8th St., 8 p.m.

"SECRETS OF ESP & HOW TO UTILIZE YOUR PSYCHIC ENERGIES" by Hal Wilcox, Oakwood Club Clubhouse, 3700 Forest Lawn and Barham Blvds., 8:15 p.m.

"PREPARATION FOR LIFE SITUATIONS" Psychodrama experience, California Institute of Socioanalysis, 1290 E. Ocean Blvd., Long Beach, 9 p.m.

Writers League Plans Meeting

The Van Nuys News (Van Nuys, California)
25 Apr 1973, Wed. Page 41

A meeting of the Professional Writers' League will be held on Saturday, at 7 p.m. at the Holland House, 347 S. Ogden Drive, Los Angeles.

The Rev. Hal Wilcox, speaker, will discuss "Secrets of ESP and How to Utilize Your Psychic Energies."

HERE AND THERE

Times-Advocate (Escondido, California)
6 Jul 1974, Tue. Page 17

REV. HAL WILCOX, founder of the Institute of Parapsychology in Los Angeles, will lecture on "Healing Technique" at 10:30 a.m. Thursday at Inspiration Hall, 434 N. Rose, Escondido. Wilcox is president of the institute, healer and teacher. He is a

graduate of Santa Monica City College and holds an architectural engineering degree. He was sent on an archaeological expedition into the Yucatan jungles and while there was shown the emerald tablets found under a headstone in the Mayan Temple of Chichen Itza. He is the author of several books.

When Zemkla calls, Wilcox answers

The San Bernardino County Sun(San Bernardino, California). 15 Oct 1977, Sat. Page 25

By JAN CLEVELAND
Sun-Telegram Staff Writer

GIANT ROCK AIRPORT — Hal Wilcox has a slightly unusual job.

During the week he works for MGM studios creating special effects for the television series "Logan's Run."

But what he does in his spare time is even more unusual.

Wilcox pGerforms mysterious projects for his outer space contact Zemkla in return for which he gets to fly in spaceships from time to time.

Wilcox said he and Zemkla have made two trips to Zemkla's planet Sello and that he has traveled in flying saucers on six different occasions.

Wilcox told his story to a small crowd of avid listeners on the first day of a three-day UFO convention being held this weekend at the tiny desert airport.

Though he was not on the agenda, his talk drew more attention than either of the day's other two speakers.

Wilcox' experiences with space dwellers began in 1952 when he was first contacted psychically by an individual he calls Fehsz.

"His method of contacting me was that I would enter a trance and then he would enter my body and speak through me. This went on for a long time, but the cross-over line came in 1961," Wilcox said.

"During a trance-contact I was told that there was a machine over my house and that my words were being broadcast up to it. I was told if I went outside I would see it and have proof that my contact was from space. I ran outside and I saw a bell-shaped craft hovering over east Los Angeles. I had no tangibility of my contacts until then," he said, tugging a straw hat that protected his face from the afternoon desert sun.

Wilcox spoke from a plywood platform, constructed with a high, white-painted wall behind it to serve as a movie screen for slide shows and films scheduled during the convention's evening hours.

Wilcox said when he was next contacted he was told he had to find others who had also been contacted and learn what they were doing with the information they were receiving. His efforts to fulfill the request took him to Japan where he said he discovered a group of people following an ancient religion based on an early space contact.

Later Wilcox relocated in Hollywood and was told he would be given "physical assistance" on his next projects.

"On day about 10 a.m. a man came to my door dressed in a white jumpsuit and looking like Burt Reynolds in the movie 'Trapeze.' He said he was Zemkla. I assumed my friends were playing a trick on me and went along with him.

"He offered to prove to me who he was and asked me to go out to the sidewalk with him. I went along, thinking it would at least be a way to get this man out of my house. When we were outside he raised his hands in the air and a bell-shaped craft came and hovered overhead. Then I believed him," Wilcox said.

Wilcox said Zemkla gave him information about a blood platelet called an indle through which people can develop their psychic abilities. He wrote a book about indles called 'Gateway to Superconsciousness: the drug experience without drugs.' He did that during the late 1960s because Zemkla told him to try to help youngsters who

(Continued on B-4, column 5)

Wilcox answers...

(Continued from Metro)

were deeply invovled in the "drug movement" at that time.

The next step was to establish a laboratory to develop super vitamins and super minerals called "plobiums."

"But I wasn't doing a very good job so I wrote a letter to Zemkla and asked him to take me to his planet so I could study and examine their way of doing things. I've flown in spacecraft six times and I have tangible documentation of it," he said.

After that Wilcox was sent on projects to Yucatan, Hawaii, Zurich and Japan. He wouldn't elaborate on the purpose of those trips. And he didn't travel by spaceship.

"I receive money from them and travel conventionally. All my projects have something to do with UFOs but usually they are just the mode of transportation, like cars are to us," he said.

Wilcox asked for a second trip to Zemkla's planet so that he could make more extensive studies there.

come out here (to the UFO conventions, stare at the sky, get sunburned and go home happy. That happened year after year, but when someone came to my front door and contacted me I didn't even believe him," Wilcox said, his voice incredulous.

Wilcox said Zemkla has at times accompanied Wilcox to UFO conventionand even been introduced.

"But he won't speak to people. He said it would interfere with the interplanetary karma. I can't understand that," Wilcox said.

The planet Sello, which Wilcox said is 7.3 light years from earth, looks like a jungle in the area he saw. Getting sick or old is a crime there and the people live in curved structures with domes or pyramid-shaped roofs.

Wilcox said most of his interplanetary flights have left Earth from a place 22 miles north of Azusa in the Las Padres National Forest.

The convention will continue Saturday and Sunday at the airport off Old Woman Springs Road near Yucca Valley.

"The first time I went I stayed about a day. The second time I stayed four days. But each time I was back here within a fraction of a second of the time that I left. That left me very confused," he said.

On the second trip Wilcox said he brought back to Earth many tangible objects that provide proof of his travels. He said the objects have been studied by the Rand Corporation and verified as being objects from another planet.

"They told me they were nothing other than what I had said they were," Wilcox said.

The middle-aged speaker said he has been the object of a half-hour long television special and appeared on the now-defunct Joe Pyne show.

Wilcox' last contact with Zemkla was in March, he said. Since then Wilcox has been working on a project to store all the information he has received from Zemkla in a computer.

"I'm up to my ears in that right now," he said.

"You know, years ago I used to

UFO buffs swap strange tales

Daily Press (Victorville, California)
16 Oct 1977, Sun. Page 1

By JOHN IDDINGS
Daily Press Staff Writer

YUCCA VALLEY — More fantastic stories and intriguing theories are being swapped at the Giant Rock Airport than probably any place in the world this weekend.

The small airport, located in a desolate desert valley 15 miles north of Yucca Valley, is the site for the 18th Southwestern Regional UFO Convention.

Only about 100 UFO buffs were on hand to kick off the three-day convention on Friday afternoon, although dozens of others began pouring in late Friday and early Saturday.

Many of those who showed up early Friday gave indications of being dedicated UFO fans. For instance, one Los Angeles woman in her mid-sixties claimed to have attended every one of the previous 17 conventions held here.

"I've been onto UFOs since I was 15 years old. That was the first time I was out of my body," she said.

She then casually told how, over 40 years ago, she was lying in her bed one night when a shaft of blue light pierced the ceiling and two strange beings appeared in the room.

They proceeded to show her how to separate herself from her physical being, she said, and float above the mundane world.

"I looked down at the world and though, 'My God, I've got to live with all that crap,'" she said, bursting into loud laughter.

Without showing any sign of skepticism a woman listening to the story nodded and claimed that her oldest son had also experienced several "astral flights."

At the airport coffee shop, four persons sat around a table sipping diet colas and discussed their theories on time and human consciousness.

"In my own life, I find that I'm experiencing a speeding up of time."

said a young man wearing a colorful robe.

He explained that he felt the level of human consciousness was increasing geometrically with each passing year, rapidly pushing humanity toward a "new world order."

On stage Friday, the stories and theories expounded by guest lecturers were no less incredible.

Hal Wilcox, a former teacher who now works as a motion picture set designer in Hollywood, told the audience that he has been in direct contact with space creatures several times. In fact, he claimed he has been off the planet earth twice as a passenger in the aliens' strange bell-shaped spacecraft.

Dan Fry, an old-timer on the UFO lecture circuit, said Friday that his own story of contact with space creatures is now so well known that it didn't even bear repeating for the seasoned buffs assembled at Giant Rock.

Instead, Fry gave a talk peppered with bits of philosophy and science about what these space creatures might be like and what their purpose might be in contacting earth people.

"I believe without a doubt that there is intelligent life on other planets," he said. "In fact, I believe that some day there might be intelligent life on this one!"

The problem with most modern scientists, said Fry, is that ". . . it never occurs to them that instead of being the observers, they may be the observed."

For those not familiar with Fry's story, he was working as an engineer at the White Sands Missile Testing Site in New Mexico where, on July 4, 1950, he claims he witnessed the landing of an unearthly device and made contact with the creatures inside. The story made national headlines at the time.

Please turn to Page 2, Col. 1

Convention in Yucca Valley
UFO buffs swap tales

Continued from Page 1

Throughout the lectures, a large auxiliary generator constantly churned and hummed in the background, supplying extra electrical power needed for the event. The sound was similar to those sometimes used to embellish space scenes in science fiction movies.

With a hot sun beating down overhead, the airport snackbac did a brisk business in beer and soft drinks. In back of the building, french rolls were piled high like a cord of firewood, soon to be split and turned into submarine sandwiches.

Jose Rogriguez, owner of the airport and organizer of the event, could be seen dashing around the area and shouting instructions to an army of teenage workers he'd recruited from Yucca Valley High School.

It was Rogriguez's first crack at organizing a UFO convention. George W. Van Tassel, who organized the previous 17 meets and who recently sold the airport to Rogriguez, was on hand Friday with pamphlets explaining the history of the Giant Rock site.

The boulder, which is seven stories high and covers 5,800 square feet of ground, was the focal point of an ancient Indian holy ground, according to Van Tassel.

A prospector named Frank Critzer dug out a small underground dwelling beneath the rock in 1930. Due to the rock's huge size, Van Tassel claims the temperature within the dwelling never varies beyond a 55-to 80-degree range since the rock stores up the summer's heat and releases it during the winter and vice versa.

A few miles south of the airport, Van Tassel has built his "Integratron," a large dome-shaped building which he says can rejuvenate any human who enters it. In addition, he said time is distroted within the structure so that those inisde can experience glimpses of both the past and future.

Activity at the convention continued right into the night on Friday and Saturday. When UFO fans weren't straining their eyes skyward in hopes of spotting a telltale flash of light, they could enjoy watching classic sci-fi films such as "The Day the Earth Stood Still" and "Chariot of the Gods."

Crowd is told 'You're the jury'...
The San Bernardino County Sun (San Bernardino, California). 23 Oct 1977, Sun. Page 27

Speaker addresses crowd at UFO convention

(Continued from Metro)

Whether you believe it or not is up to you. You're the jury."

For the most part, the jury was very open-minded. A few among the approximately 400 persons present dared to be cynical during some of the lectures, but they soon were soon shushed into silence.

For the believers, the convention (the first since 1969 to be held at the little "interplanetary" desert air strip) was glorious. They could talk about meeting people from outer space and no one threatened to call the men in white coats.

When speaker Hal Wilcox finished relating his tale of travel by spaceship to the planet Sello, dozens of people flocked to him, wanting to buy his books and hear more about his space contact, Zemkla.

Although the much-discussed space people failed to make an appearance, those attending the three-day-long gathering were not dismayed. They knew the space people had been to Giant Rock before and if though they missed the convention, they would surely come another time.

According to George Van Tassel, a desert dweller considered to be the dean of the UFO believers, the extraterrestrial visits to Giant Rock began in 1953 while he was operating the airport.

The visits developed from experiments in mental telepathy Van Tassel and several other people were conducting at that time, he said.

"We were trying to use mental could move objects all over the room. All the stuff you're seeing them do now with telekinesis — we were doing that years ago."

The outer space visitors somehow contacted Van Tassel through his mental telepathy exercises and eventually landed at Giant Rock, he told the conventioneers.

"We were sleeping outside one night and the spaceship came down and landed in a rough area about 100 yards from the rock," Van Tassel said.

"A man got out and walked over to me and woke me up. He asked me if I'd like a tour of the ship and I said 'yes.' The ship had a hole in the bottom and they lifted me in with a gravity nullifying beam and showed me around," he said.

Van Tassel said the ship and the people very much resembled those depicted in a science fiction film called "The Day The Earth Stood Still," one of two movies shown at the convention.

"They asked me if I would like to do something for the people. I thought about my three daughters and my grandchildren and I had to answer yes. You don't do these things because you really want to, but for the future generations," he said.

The space beings, to whom Van Tassel refers as "these people" or simply "they," told him to build a nonmetallic structure at least 18 feet in diameter. Van Tassel responded by constructing a large, white-domed building he calls the "Integraton."

traterrestrial visits to Giant Rock began in 1953 while he was operating the airport.

The visits developed from experiments in mental telepathy Van Tassel and several other people were conducting at that time, he said.

"We were trying to use mental telepathy as a means of communication because at that time we didn't have telephones out here. It was a long way from here to town and we thought if we could communicate without making the trip it would make things a lot easier. The experiments worked, too.

"We got to the point where we

The space beings, to whom Van Tassel refers as "these people" or simply "they," told him to build a nonmetallic structure at least 18 feet in diameter. Van Tassel responded by constructing a large, white-domed building he calls the "Integraton."

The building is something of a landmark around the tiny desert community of Landers, where it stands on property Van Tassel has donated to what he has named the College of Universal Wisdom.

The strange looking structure seemed an appropriate introduction to the UFO convention, standing as it does at the entrance to a dirt road leading to the airport. Many visitors slowed their campers and recreational vehicles to study the building and a nearby observatory as they passed.

Van Tassel said the Integraton is the result of hundreds of hours of research based on information provided by "these people" and is designed to prolong human life.

Through a complicated process of ionization, Van Tassel said the machine, which may be operable next year, will be capable of extending human life by 50 to 80 years. His listeners understood the aging Van Tassel's unspoken message that he would be the first volunteer for the rejuvenation experiments.

With Van Tassel as their leader, the convention-goers and speakers comprised a somewhat elitist group.

They were the most dedicated of UFO buffs and had heard all the flying saucer stories that could be told. If they hadn't heard them they wouldn't admit to it.

Dan Fry, once an employe at the White Sands Proving Grounds in Las Cruces, N.M., told the crowd he had seen and touched a flying saucer there.

"I can't believe there is anyone out there (in the audience) who hasn't already heard the story dozens of times, so I won't bore you by telling it again," he told the group. "Is there anyone out there who hasn't heard the story? Raise your hands."

seeing flying saucers," he said with a grim smile.

"I finally got close enough to touch the surface, which I found to be several degrees warmer than the air temperature. It was extremely smooth and slippery. Words cannot explain what that surface felt like. I couldn't produce any friction when I rubbed my hand across it."

But just when Fry's account was getting interesting, he was told the next speaker had finally arrived. So he left the stand without finishing the story.

Again there were a few grumbles from the audience, but no one chased after Fry to hear what happened with his spaceship.

The convention audience of about 400 people was considerably smaller than the 6,000 promoters predicted would attend. And a large portion of that audience was made up of persons wearing press passes. At least two crews filmed the convention for a documentary and a television program. A number of newspapers and magazines were also represented.

material.

That was after he had discussed the indisputable reality of flying saucers, said they were not actually ships but permanent homes for space wanderers and reported that human beings eventually will emigrate away from Earth (threatened as it is with ecological disaster) onto similar space homes that will be much safer than the endangered planet.

Fry, a verbose man, seemed to do a lion's-share of the speaking during the Friday and Saturday meetings, but there was a reason for that. He was the man the organizers counted on to fill in for a number of guest speakers who didn't show up.

He was called on Oct. 14 when Orfeo Angelucci did not arrive as scheduled. Then the next day Fry was asked to fill in for Travis Walton, who was to tell of his recent five-day kidnaping from Snowflake, Ariz., by space people. Through a foul-up in communications, according to the organizers, Walton didn't show up.

Toward the end of his Friday speech, Fry finally began to talk about his Las Cruces sighting.

"On the evening of July 3, 1950, I saw a device with no propellers, no jet stream and no wing surfaces descend onto the desert. I knew there was nothing like that on Earth.

"At that time I was at the forefront of our space work — actually at that time they were just space hopes — and I wasn't ready to accept the existence of these objects either," Fry said.

"It landed at zero velocity and I knew it could not have been anything built on Earth. That realization gave me the strong urge to be somewhere else, and I didn't much care where that someplace else was. But I didn't do anything," he said.

Fry was the only speaker to admit an initial fear of a flying saucer.

"I just stood there, torn between the instinct to flee and the urge to find out more about the object. I found myself approaching it a step at a time, a step at a time," Fry recalled.

He said the silvery vehicle was about 16 feet high with no door and no windows.

"After I took a half a dozen steps toward the object, I began to think of rushing back to the base to get some others to come out there with me — but I realized I could lose my job if it wasn't there when I came back.

"Accuracy and good judgment were essential to my job and companies like mine don't hire mentally unbalanced people who talk about seeing flying saucers," he said with a grim smile.

"I finally got close enough to touch the surface, which I found to be several degrees warmer than the air temperature. It was extremely smooth and slippery. Words cannot explain what that surface felt like. I couldn't produce any friction when I rubbed my hand across it."

But just when Fry's account was getting interesting, he was told the next speaker had finally arrived. So he left the stand without finishing the story.

Again there were a few grumbles from the audience, but no one chased after Fry to hear what happened with his spaceship.

The convention audience of about 400 people was considerably smaller than the 6,000 promoters predicted would attend. And a large portion of that audience was made up of persons wearing press passes. At least two crews filmed the convention for a documentary and a television program. A number of newspapers and magazines were also represented.

But there weren't many complaints about the missing speakers voiced by the convention-goers, except perhaps that the site offered very little protection from the hot desert sun. By early afternoon most of the audience was huddled up against a large boulder-covered hill, seeking the meager shade provided by rocks.

Some brought umbrellas and awnings for shade, while others sat under the patio roof of a small restaurant, totally out of sight of the speakers but still within earshot. Even they seemed pleased to be there, possibly because their seats offered easy access to the cold drinks sold in the small restaurant.

"Isn't this just wonderful," one woman asked happily.

She sported a beet-red sunburn but it didn't daunt her.

"I think this is just the most fascinating thing I have ever heard. It's just great to be here," she said, apparently summing up the feelings of most of the UFO watchers in attendance.

Nomad's Notebook
Convention Is Way Out One
By Walt Wiley

The Sacramento Bee (Sacramento, California)
07 Nov 1977, Mon. Page 3

I DON'T KNOW WHAT I should've expected, but I was completely surprised by what I found when I attended a UFO convention not long ago.

A publicity blurb came in the mail, announcing that 6,000 people were expected to show up at a spot called Giant Rock Interplanetary Airport in the Mojave Desert 50 miles north of Palm Springs.

There was a telephone number on the announcement, so I called and got a woman who was handling publicity for the event.

She told me, "Monitoring craft from Saturn should be there."

Then she went on, "The Universe is law and order all the way; there's good guys and bad guys, and the dark powers have force too.

"It's time the people on this planet knew the way this is linking up so they can act before it's too late."

THAT WAS ALL HEADY STUFF FOR ME. I wouldn't know a space man if he bit me, though I have known some people who could've passed for Martians — or Saturnians.

I decided to see for myself. I flew down there, rented a car and headed out.

Giant Rock is out in the middle of nowhere.

You leae the pavement about 10 miles before you get there, and you know you've arrived when you see the biggest boulder you've ever seen. It's seven stories tall, I was told, and there's a parlor tunneled out of the ground beneath it.

THE CROWD — NOWHERE NEAR 6,000 — sure didn't look like a band of Martians. They were about as normal-looking a bunch as you could find. The older ones could've been Rotarians or insurance agents; the younger were typical young people.

And I couldn't find a one among them who'd own up to being a die-hard UFO believer.

Repeatedly, I would ask folk what might be their thoughts on UFOs. They answered, time and again, that they were mildly

UFO buffs gather at the Giant Rock Interplanetary Airport.

interested, curious about what the speakers might have to say.

But admission to the event was $15 per person, and the drive was no casual undertaking. Some of the cars had even come from places as far as Washington and Texas. Mildly interested?

A woman sitting near me during a lecture snorted out loud: "Can you believe this crap?"

But after the lecture, she was back behind the stage talking intently with the lecturer, exchanging notes on slips of paper torn from the program.

"Aha! Closet Believer!" I thought as I watched her.

THERE WERE TWO GROUPS, more or less, in the crowd: older and younger.

The older group — some into their 90s — seemed interested in the speakers who talked about a near-eternal life span for human beings.

The speakers said they had traveled aboard space craft to different planets where the residents lived to ages "on the order of 900 earth years."

I guess this was pretty good news to people of advanced age — the idea that maybe they were only beginning their lives.

The younger crowd was interested in gadgets and machines — especially things that run on free magnetic power.

Pyramids made of poles were popular with this bunch. One young lady told me the small open pyramid she wore on her head kept her cool in the sun, even though it made no shade.

ONE LECTURER TALKED OF HIS FRIEND, Zem-Kla, who escorted him to his native planet, Celo, where the people have attained an existence which is just about perfect.

Another lecturer did some bizarre things with numbers to prove a link among space travel, the speed of light, UFO sightings and a grid of mysterious antennas on houses all over the island of New Zealand.

All this was beyond my feeble brain's capacity to swallow, let alone digest. I was missing it.

And the speakers apparently felt no need to bridge a gap between the stuff they were saying and something I could understand — such as ordinary high school physics.

They were talking to UFO believers. It was as if a bible scholar were discussing some fine point of theology with a group of Christians.

There could have been disagreement, but the basic creed was a common ground of understanding.

It was shop talk. And even UFO shop talk is brutally dull.

It was no more interesting for an outsider than a convention of, say, paint dealers.

I DIDN'T STAY FOR THE WHOLE AFFAIR, but as I was leaving I made one last attempt at getting a handle on things.

The master of ceremonies was a San Diego commercial pilot who had shown me some photographs of a cigar-shaped blur he said was a UFO.

As I left, I asked him how well the contentions of one of the speakers fit in with mainstream UFO thinking.

"He's really radical fringe," the MC replied. "But people were laughing at that guy 30 years ago, calling him a nut. In those days he was predicting he'd live to see men walk on the moon."

UFO buffs stage their own close encounter

By DENNIS KELLY
Sun Staff Writer

The San Bernardino County Sun (San Bernardino, California)

11 May 1982, Tue. Page 7

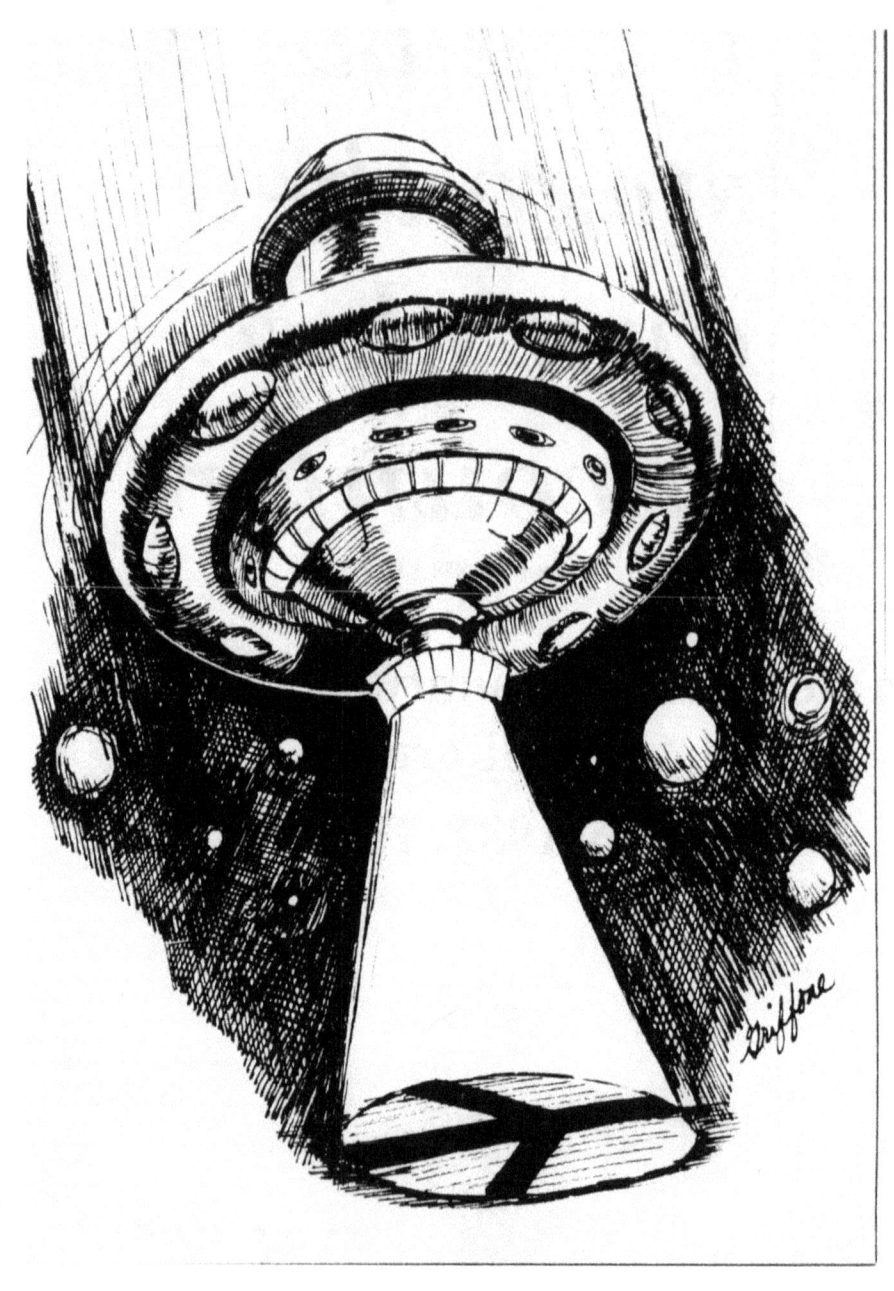

Sun Staff Writer

UPLAND — Even if you don't believe all those folks who say they've had contact with beings from other planets, it's pretty hard to knock the message they've brought back from the aliens.

It's almost always in the form of a call for peace, a warning to stop the nuclear arms build-up that could lead to the destruction of the planet Earth — just as so many of the aliens reportedly say their own planets were destroyed with such technology.

That was the underlying theme of the Flying Saucer Convention here this weekend sponsored by Understanding Inc., a non-profit group founded by Dr. Daniel Fry, a retired rocket technician and a UFO (unidentified flying object) contactee.

This was a gathering of people who not only are convinced that aliens from other planets in other galaxies have visited earth, but they are also people who say they have had contact with some of those beings.

The approximately 100 people who attended the two-day convention at the Astara Center here were among friends. They could listen to about a dozen speakers who updated their findings from contacts with other beings and they could talk about their own experiences without fear of public derision.

They talked about seeing balls of light go through living rooms, flying saucers hovering over garages with beams of light, aliens communicating with earthlings by taking over their bodies and "transchanneling" — and no one in the crowd batted an eye.

Bill Hamilton, of Phoenix, Ariz., one of the convention organizers, admitted there is still great skepticism among the public even though the latest Gallup poll shows the "majority" of the U.S. population "accepts UFO reality."

U.S. population "accepts UFO reality."

"There's still a segment of the public, maybe 40 percent, that considers the subject of flying saucers either lunacy or a threat to their religious or spiritual beliefs," said Hamilton, a computer programmer and UFO investigator.

Hamilton's own talk touched on how, in his contacts with aliens, "the basis for all knowledge was revealed to me.

"The universe is based on one idea and only one idea," he said. And that was the circle, a "point expanded in an arc at a constant rate."

This convention was one of several that have been held in various communities by Understanding Inc. since the end of the conventions that were held at Giant Rock "Interplanetary" Airport outside Yucca Valley. The conventions there came to a halt with the death of George Van Tassel, operator of the airport and a man called the dean of the UFO movement.

The speakers didn't bother trying to prove to this audience that UFOs exist. Rather, their talks were updates on what they had learned from their contacts.

One speaker was Hal Wilcox, a former school music teacher now in the motion picture business doing special effects, who said he has made several trips to another planet with aliens. Wilcox is now in the process of trying to help people set up combinations of radio equipment and home computers that will allow earth residents to tune into the Interplanetary Cultural Exchange (ICE). It will link about 50 planets so they may share knowledge.

"The benefit will be mostly personal in spiritual development," Wilcox told a reporter after his talk. Wilcox said that the lesson other civilizations have learned and wish to share with earth is that they spent too much time speeding along their mechanical and physical evolution and not enough on the spiritual side.

Wilcox said he has learned this information since his contact with a being named "Fahsz" outside his home in Los Angeles in October, 1961. From a space vehicle hovering above his home, Fahsz used Wilcox' body to "transchannel," communicate through the earthling.

After that he was "physically taken" from the University of Southern California campus in 1964 to Fahsz' home planet, Selo. He made a second trip in 1968, brought back evidence that he had been to the planet, and has passed every test the FBI and CIA could give him, he said. His contact on both those trips was a being named "Zemkla," and some other aliens who looked much like humans except that they were healthy.

He said the message he's been given is that — with computers and radios — America now has the "equal opportunity" and the tools to complete this Interplanetary Cultural Exchange and now must get on with "using it or losing it."

"I was told, 'You have all the tools. You have all the material. All you need to do is complete the project.'"

Hamilton, of Phoenix, spoke about his investigations of the Brian Scott case and how that affected his own life. Scott, a design engineer, and a friend reportedly were abducted in March, 1971, outside Apache Junction, Ariz. They were lifted into a spacecraft and encountered three to four "hulking, elephantine beings" each about nine feet tall.

Scott was then shown images of the aliens' home planet as it looked before its destruction.

Two years later, Scott returned to the same site and was abducted again. Hamilton said the purpose of Scott's adbuctions was to bring about a mental transformation in Scott to enable him to bring the aliens' technology to earth so that it could help bring about peace.

The message that aliens bring to most contactees is that they have seen the expansion of earth's technology "in a destructive direction," Hamilton said. "The second thing is they seem to be building toward some future event that may have spiritual, social and physical consequences to people on earth."

Does that mean the Second Coming, he was asked?

"We don't know," Hamilton said.

The speakers weren't the only ones who said they had had contacts with alien beings, however.

There was, for instance, Frank Duarte from Pico Rivera, who said he had 21 meetings with space visitors between 1968 and 1972.

"I came out to buy some pictures from a fellow

(Please see UFO, A-9)

UFO...

(Continued from A-7)

who got NASA prints before they were classified," he told a reporter over lunch. "They are pictures of buildings on the moon that look like oil derricks, and buildings and bridges."

Duarte said the public is still skeptical of people claiming to have had contact with space creatures. He said his own mother put him in a mental institution at age 18. "Part of it" was because of his claims of seeing aliens.

"They all want proof," Duarte said. "The general public has this attitude, 'What are you (the aliens) going to do for us? How many food stamps will you give us?'"

Duarte said he wanted to help the aliens and that his assignment was to build a space landing platform "somewhere in Nebraska."

"We don't want everybody to know about it," he said.

Marion Wagner, an elderly woman from Santa Monica, came to the convention because, she said, she had an experience in the early 1950s when a space craft hovered over the garage of her house.

It beamed "enormous" rays of light down to the ground.

The people who don't believe in UFO's "don't know what they're talking about," she said. The aliens have an important message to "expand love instead of hate."

"If we're lifted up, then we lift all mankind," she said.

Dr. Fry, in his keynote address to the convention Saturday, didn't talk about his contacts with alien beings in the 1950s in the White Sands area of New Mexico. Yet, those contacts were the reason he began Understanding Inc.

"When I first began to speak about the visits to this planet, oftentimes, someone would say, 'Oh, Dr. Fry, do you really believe there are intelligent beings on other planets?' My only reply is there is no doubt whatever that they exist and this belief gives me the hope there may some day be intelligent life on this one," he said as the audience broke into laughter and applause.

He said the purpose of his organization was to promote — as the name says — the kind of understanding that can help prevent wars.

Dry has proposed a conference of world leaders to give as complete a study of the social sciences — the principles behind human relationships — as has been given to the physical sciences.

"Our religious leaders say, 'Love your neighbor.' Unfortunately, they don't tell us how to go about it," he said.

"Unfortunately, love is an emotion that is not subject to the will."

If a rich man offers you $1 million to love a person you can't stand, he said, you can go through the motions of love and respect, "but in your heart there would be no difference."

Peace, Fry said, is not a goal that can be pursued as though it is a separate entity. It is a by-product of understanding.

"It (peace) is not a treasure which you can find by digging," Fry said. "Peace is a by-product of complete understanding between man and his fellow man, between state and state, and by the powers that govern."

Fry said he keeps talking about the contacts he's made with alien beings because inhabitants of earth haven't taken the message seriously yet.

A10 EVENING JOURNAL
Tuesday ••• May 11, 1982

The contact sport of 'UFO-ing'

By Dennis Kelly
Gannett News Service

The News Journal (Wilmington, Delaware)
11 May 1982, Tue. Page 10

UPLAND, Calif. — Even if you don't believe all those folks who say they've had contact with beings from other planets, it's pretty hard to knock the message they've brought back from the aliens.

It's almost always in the form of a call for peace, a warning to stop the nuclear arms buildup that could lead to the destruction of the planet Earth — just as so many of the aliens reportedly say their own planets were destroyed with such technology.

That was the underlying theme of the Flying Saucer Convention over the weekend sponsored by Understanding Inc., a non-profit group founded by Dr. Daniel Fry, a retired rocket technician and a UFO (unidentified flying object) contactee.

It was a gathering of people who not only are convinced that aliens from other planets in other galaxies have visited Earth, but they are also people who say they have had contact with some of those beings.

The approximately 100 people who attended the two-day convention here were among friends. They could listen to about a dozen speakers who updated their findings from contacts with other beings and they could talk about their own experiences without fear of public derision.

Bill Hamilton, computer programmer and UFO investigator from Phoenix, Ariz., one of the convention organizers, admitted there is still great skepticism among the public even though the latest Gallup poll shows the "majority" of the U.S. population "accepts UFO reality."

The message that aliens bring to most contactees is that they have seen the expansion of earth's technology "in a destructive direction," Hamilton said. Another speaker, Hal Wilcox, a former school music teacher now in the motion picture business doing special effects, said he has made several trips to another planet with aliens. Wilcox is trying to help people set up combinations of radio equipment and home computers that will allow Earth residents to tune into the Interplanetary Cultural Exchange. It will link about 50 planets so they may share knowledge.

"The benefit will be mostly personal in spiritual development," Wilcox told a reporter after his talk. Wilcox said that the lesson other civilizations have learned and wish to share with Earth is that they spent too much time speeding along their mechanical and physical evolution and not enough on the spiritual side.

Wilcox said he has learned this information since his contact with a being named "Fahsz" outside his home in Los Angeles in October 1961. From a space vehicle hovering above his home, Fahsz used Wilcox' body to "transchannel," communicate through the earthling.

People

UFO conventioneers swap tales of alien encounters

The Californian (Salinas, California).
11 May 1982, Tue. Page 18

UPLAND (GNS) — Even if you don't believe all those folks who say they've had contact with beings from other planets, it's pretty hard to knock the message they've brought back from the aliens.

It's almost always in the form of a call for peace, a warning to stop the nuclear arms buildup that could lead to the destruction of the planet Earth — just as so many of the aliens reportedly say their own planets were destroyed with such technology.

That was the underlying theme of the Flying Saucer Convention over the weekend sponsored by Understanding Inc., a non-profit group founded by Dr. Daniel Fry, a retired rocket technician and a UFO (unidentified flying object) contactee.

It was a gathering of people who not only are convinced that aliens from other planets in other galaxies have visited Earth, but they are also people who say they have had contact with some of those beings.

The approximately 100 people who attended the two-day convention here were among friends. They could listen to about a dozen speakers who updated their findings from contacts with other beings and they could talk about their own experiences without fear of public derision.

They talked about seeing balls of light go through living rooms, flying saucers with beams of light hovering over garages, aliens communicating with earthlings by taking over their bodies and "trans-channeling" — and no one in the crowd batted an eye.

Bill Hamilton, computer programmer and UFO investigator from Phoenix, Ariz., one of the convention organizers, admitted there is still great skepticism among the public even though the latest Gallup poll shows the "majority" of the U.S. population "accepts UFO reality."

Hamilton spoke about his investigations of the Brian Scott case and how that affected his own life. Scott, a design engineer, and a friend reportedly were abducted in March 1971, outside Apache Junction, Ariz. They were lifted into a spacecraft and encountered three to four "hulking, elephantine beings," each about 9 feet tall.

Scott was then shown images of the aliens' home planet as it looked before its destruction.

Two years later, Scott returned to the same site and was abducted again. Hamilton said the purpose of Scott's abductions was to bring about a mental transformation in Scott to enable him to bring the aliens' technology to Earth so that it could help bring about peace.

The message that aliens bring to most contactees is that they have seen the expansion of earth's technology "in a destructive direction," Hamilton said. Another speaker, Hal Wilcox, a former school music teacher now in the motion picture business doing special effects, said he has made several trips to another planet with aliens. Wilcox is trying to help people set up combinations of radio equipment and home computers that will allow Earth residents to tune into the Interplanetary Cultural Exchange. It will link about 50 planets so they may share knowledge.

"The benefit will be mostly personal in spiritual development," Wilcox told a reporter after his talk. Wilcox said that the lesson other civilizations have learned and wish to share with Earth is that they spent too much time speeding along their mechanical and physical evolution and not enough on the spiritual side.

Wilcox said he has learned this information since his contact with a being named "Fahsz" outside his home in Los Angeles in October 1961. From a space vehicle hovering above his home, Fahsz used Wilcox' body to "transchannel," communicate through the earthling.

After that he was "physically taken" from the University of Southern California campus in 1964 to Fahsz' home planet, Selo.

Calendar Lectures
The Los Angeles Times (Los Angeles, California)
18 Dec 1983, Sun. Page 298

MY PHYSICAL UFO EXPERIENCES (Church of the Inner Light, 1557 S. Barrington Ave., West Los Angeles, 11 a.m., 277-2613). Dr. Hal Wilcox.

CALENDAR

The Los Angeles Times (Los Angeles, California)

18 Dec 1983, Sun. Page 298

LECTURES

TODAY

MY PHYSICAL UFO EXPERIENCES (Church of the Inner Light, 1557 S. Barrington Ave., West Los Angeles, 11 a.m., 277-2613). Dr. Hal Wilcox.

The best... THE MARGARINE CHRONICLES
LA Weekly (Los Angeles, California)
30 Sep 1993, Thu. Page 116

the best ...

THE MARGARINE CHRONICLES

Hal Wilcox's UFO Experiences Dinner at Denny's. The audience at the table, with the exception of Rachel from Chatsworth, is captivated. In her 60s, rocking back and forth in a *faux*-Penney's suit, she's talking to herself and to the "people" who lodged an implant in her brain. Periodically the conversation digresses as she slaps the table and whispers, "Protons." It's Friday night at Hollywood's rock & roll Denny's. A plastic ID badge reading "Dr. Hal Wilcox, Physical Contactee" identifies the heavyset man who works the Formica corner booth week after week. The "doctor" does most of the talking in these introductory meetings, punctuating his banter with tiny trajectories of clam chowder. Anyone's welcome to come by and discuss the UFO topic *du jour* over a Chicken and Ham Slam. Lately, discussions have drifted toward time-line travel and office sightings of 9-foot space aliens. In the next booth, a party of original L. Ron Hubbard apostles, aged and world-weary beyond any further discussion of *Battleship Earth*, struggle with their sugar packets. *7:30-9:30 p.m. Fridays at Denny's, 5751 Sunset Blvd., Hollywood; (213) 464-8435.* (Mary Melton)

www.ingramcontent.com/pod-product-compliance
Lightning Source LLC
Chambersburg PA
CBHW080453170426
43196CB00016B/2791